D1605236

WORLD HISTORY

American Counterculture of the 1960s

By Richard Brownell

LUCENT BOOKS
A part of Gale, Cengage Learning

GALE
CENGAGE Learning

Detroit • New York • San Francisco • New Haven, Conn • Waterville, Maine • London

LIBRARY OF CONGRESS CATALOGING-IN-PUBLICATION DATA

Brownell, Richard.
    American counterculture of the 1960s / by Richard Brownell.
        p. cm. -- (World history)
    Includes bibliographical references and index.
    ISBN 978-1-4205-0263-3 (hardcover)
    1. United States--Social conditions--1960-1980. 2. Counterculture--United States--History--20th century. 3. Protest movements--United States--History--20th century. I. Title.
    HN59.B78 2010
    306'.1--dc22
                                                                2010010503

Lucent Books
27500 Drake Rd.
Farmington Hills, MI 48331

ISBN-13: 978-1-4205-0263-3
ISBN-10: 1-4205-0263-8

Printed in the United States of America
1 2 3 4 5 6 7 14 13 12 11 10

Printed by Bang Printing, Brainerd, MN, 1st Ptg., 09/2010

Contents

Foreword

Each year, on the first day of school, nearly every history teacher faces the task of explaining why his or her students should study history. Many reasons have been given. One is that lessons exist in the past from which contemporary society can benefit and learn. Another is that exploration of the past allows us to see the origins of our customs, ideas, and institutions. Concepts such as democracy, ethnic conflict, or even things as trivial as fashion or mores, have historical roots.

Reasons such as these impress few students, however. If anything, these explanations seem remote and dull to young minds. Yet history is anything but dull. And therein lies what is perhaps the most compelling reason for studying history: History is filled with great stories. The classic themes of literature and drama—love and sacrifice, hatred and revenge, injustice and betrayal, adversity and overcoming adversity – fill the pages of history books, feeding the imagination as well as any of the great works of fiction do.

The story of the Children's Crusade, for example, is one of the most tragic in history. In 1212 Crusader fever hit Europe. A call went out to the pope that all good Christians should journey to Jerusalem to drive out the hated Muslims and return the city to Christian control.

Heeding the call, thousands of children made the journey. Parents bravely allowed many children to go, and entire communities were inspired by the faith of these small Crusaders. Unfortunately, many boarded ships captained by slave traders, who enthusiastically sold the children into slavery as soon as they arrived at their destination. Thousands died from disease, exposure, and starvation on the long march across Europe to the Mediterranean Sea. Others perished at sea.

Another story, from a modern and more familiar place, offers a soul-wrenching view of personal humiliation but also the ability to rise above it. Hatsuye Egami was one of 110,000 Japanese Americans sent to internment camps during World War II. "Since yesterday we Japanese have ceased to be human beings," he wrote in his diary. "We are numbers. We are no longer Egamis, but the number 23324. A tag with that number is on every trunk, suitcase and bag. Tags, also, on our breasts." Despite such dehumanizing treatment, most internees worked hard to control their bitterness. They created workable communities inside the camps and demonstrated again and again their loyalty as Americans.

These are but two of the many stories from history that can be found in the pages of the Lucent Books World History series. All World History titles rely on sound research and verifiable evidence, and all give students a clear sense of time, place, and chronology through maps and time-lines as well as text.

All titles include a wide range of authoritative perspectives that demonstrate the complexity of historical interpretation and sharpen the reader's critical thinking skills. Formally documented quotations and annotated bibliographies enable students to locate and evaluate sources, often instantaneously via the Internet, and serve as valuable tools for further research and debate.

Finally, Lucent's World History titles present rousing good stories, featuring vivid primary source quotations drawn from unique, sometimes obscure sources such as diaries, public records, and contemporary chronicles. In this way, the voices of participants and witnesses as well as important biographers and historians bring the study of history to life. As we are caught up in the lives of others, we are reminded that we too are characters in the ongoing human saga, and we are better prepared for our own roles.

Important Dates in the Time of

August 6, 1960
Cuban dictator Fidel Castro confiscates American and foreign-owned businesses in Cuba.

February 20, 1962
John Glenn becomes first American to orbit Earth.

October 16, 1964
Communist China test detonates its first atomic bomb.

May 5, 1961
Alan Shepard becomes the first American in space.

November 22, 1963
President John F. Kennedy is assassinated in Dallas, Texas.

1960	1961	1962	1963	1964

August 13, 1961
Soviets and East Germans begin construction of the Berlin Wall, raising Cold War tensions with the West.

October 22, 1962
The U.S. discovery of Soviet missiles in Cuba leads to a tense standoff, bringing America and the U.S.S.R. to the brink of nuclear war.

December 10, 1964
Martin Luther King is awarded the Nobe Peace Prize.

August 5, 1963
The United States, the United Kingdom, and the Soviet Union sign an atmospheric nuclear test ban treaty.

American Counterculture of the 1960s

June 1, 1967
The Beatles release their album *Sgt. Pepper's Lonely Hearts Club Band*.

June 3, 1968
Andy Warhol is shot by radical feminist Valerie Solanas and barely survives the attack.

July 20, 1969
American Neil Armstrong becomes the first man to walk on the moon.

June 13, 1966
The U.S. Supreme Court rules in *Miranda v. Arizona* that police must inform suspects of their rights before questioning.

October 2, 1967
Thurgood Marshall sworn in as first African American Supreme Court justice.

October 2, 1968
Several students are killed by police during a protest in Mexico City. The extent of the deaths is never known.

1966	1967	1968	1969

March 16, 1968
U.S. soldiers murder 504 Vietnamese civilians in the My Lai Massacre. Support for the war plummets when the incident becomes public a year later.

September 2, 1969
Ho Chi Minh, leader of Communist North Vietnam, dies at age 79.

June 5, 1967
The Six-Day War begins between Israel and several Arab nations. Israel readily wins the conflict.

October 9, 1967
Marxist revolutionary Ernesto "Che" Guevara is killed while trying to incite a communist rebellion in Bolivia.

Marching to a Different Beat

The United States was in a period of dramatic economic growth in the 1950s, and many people saw their standard of living rise to a level they never thought possible. Victory in World War II had made America the most powerful country in the world, and its industrial base produced goods at a pace that no other country could match. The gross domestic product for the country rose from $273 billion in 1950 to $517 billion in 1960. Home ownership became more affordable, and newlyweds and young families took advantage of improved economic conditions to move out of the cities to the rapidly growing suburbs. The 20 percent rise in real wages during that time allowed people to purchase refrigerators, televisions, and labor saving devices such as washing machines and dishwashers. Automobiles also became more affordable and more prevalent. And a college education, once considered attainable only by the wealthy, was now within reach of the average American, opening up opportunities for better careers and higher wages.

This new affluence and the modern American culture that it created did not reach everyone. Women who were housewives and mothers lived with the advantages that the culture afforded them, but they were never expected to want more than the traditional role that prevented them from living independently or pursuing their own careers. Blacks in the South were subject to racist laws that prevented them from voting, earning a living comparable to whites, or even using the same public facilities as whites. Other minorities, such as Hispanics and American Indians, likewise found the opportunities that were being afforded to large segments of the society eluded them.

Another group did not share in the affluent American culture, but for them it was by choice. They were mostly young writers, artists, and wanderers who rejected a society in which the majority enjoyed owning televisions, washing machines, and air conditioners. They believed that most Americans had become willing prisoners to the lifestyles they maintained. These younger people wanted no part of the affluence and materialism of the 1950s, so they created a lifestyle that was separate and distinct.

The Beats

This group of young artists was known collectively as the Beat Generation. They defined themselves through their art, and the themes of their work often embraced travel, non-conformity, and spontaneity; they frequently questioned the values of the larger society and the government.

The term *Beat* has often been attributed to Jack Kerouac, a writer of that period.

Writer Jack Kerouac and poet Allen Ginsberg became the best-known Beat figures of the time, consistently pushing the boundaries of their art while embracing spontaneity and non-conformity.

Kerouac noted that to be "beat" was to be poor and downtrodden, but free and beatific, or blissfully happy. Novelist Joyce Johnson, who knew Kerouac, associated the meaning of the Beat Generation with the characters in Kerouac's book, *On the Road*, which came to symbolize the period. "Their main goal in life was to 'know time,' which they could achieve by packing as much intensity as possible into each moment. [They] didn't have houses with mortgages—they had wheels. They didn't worry about hanging on to 9 to 5 jobs … they didn't care about achieving respectability."[1]

Kerouac, fellow writer William Burroughs, and poet Allen Ginsberg became the best-known figures of the time. These three men, along with many others like them, traveled the country and often gathered in the coffee shops and jazz clubs of San Francisco or New York City's Greenwich Village, where they shared their art and their ideas. They experimented with drugs, alternative lifestyles, and frequently pushed the boundaries of their art and the law.

Ginsberg's epic poem *Howl* was considered obscene for its use of foul language and sexual imagery, and his publisher Lawrence Ferlinghetti was arrested in 1957 for printing and distributing it. Similarly, William Burroughs's 1959 novel, *Naked Lunch*, was banned in the United States. The First Amendment prevailed in both cases and the works, like *On the Road*, gradually found an audience.

Inspiring a New Generation

On the Road, Howl, and *Naked Lunch* eventually became American literary classics, but at the time they were published, the broad critical and commercial response was mixed. The writing of the Beats was best characterized as spontaneous and boundless, and it did not fit any widely accepted style of literature.

Kerouac's writing method was so rapid and energetic that he would tape together sheets of typing paper into long scrolls in advance so that he would not have to stop to change pages in the typewriter when he was writing. He wrote the original manuscript for *On the Road* in three weeks. It had an almost chaotic tempo, and the first draft was virtually unpublishable. Burroughs, who battled morphine addiction through much of the 1950s, wrote in a nonlinear fashion and often stacked his manuscript pages unnumbered and at random. As a result, the larger literary market frequently dismissed his work as muddled and incomprehensible.

The reaction to the art and lifestyle of the Beats was notable in three distinct ways. First, they were ridiculed. Herb Caen, a widely read columnist for the *San Francisco Chronicle* referred to them in 1958 as *beatniks*. This term, inspired by the Russian satellite named *Sputnik*, implied that they were un-American, and the Beats themselves thought the term was insulting because it trivialized them. *Life* Magazine characterized the Beats as "talkers, loafers, passive little con men, lonely eccentrics, mom-haters, cophaters … writers who cannot write, painters who cannot paint."[2]

The Beats were also imitated. Berets, black turtlenecks, goatees, and skintight pants became high fashion for a group of people who attended Beat poetry readings and music sessions. These styles came to symbolize the Beats themselves, but most sincere members of the Beat Generation never really wore this style of clothing. Films that either halfheartedly attempted to celebrate the Beat lifestyle or grossly misrepresented it were popular for a time. The self-styled Beat character Maynard G. Krebs on the television comedy "The Many Loves of Dobie Gillis" helped make the show a hit by satirizing beatniks for comic relief.

Most importantly, the Beats inspired a group of young people who were not directly connected to their scene on either the East or West Coast. The writings of Kerouac and Ginsberg influenced young musicians, such as Bob Dylan and John Lennon, and budding writers, such as Ken Kesey and Hunter S. Thompson.

The writings of the Beats spoke directly to an American generation that was coming of age and had grown restless with the quiet, staid lifestyle of its parents. The older generation did not want to risk the comfort that came with the relative peace and prosperity that had eluded America for two decades. The youth who had not experienced the poverty of the Great Depression or the strict rationing of goods and services during World War II did not appreciate this sentiment. In their view society was stifling true freedom of thought and action and unfairly distributing the riches of the American society. The younger generation wanted change, and some of them were willing to go to great lengths to achieve it.

Chapter One

Exploring a New Frontier

The 1960s opened with a promise of change. President John F. Kennedy noted in his inaugural address on January 20, 1961, "The torch has been passed to a new generation of Americans ... unwilling to witness or permit the slow undoing of those human rights to which this Nation has always been committed."[3] Kennedy's election the previous November had been one of the closest in American history, earning him a margin of victory of about 100,000 votes out of 68 million cast, yet it symbolized a new beginning for a new generation.

Kennedy, the youngest man ever elected president, replaced Dwight D. Eisenhower, the oldest man ever to serve in the White House. This was important, because it signified a fresh perspective in America's leadership at a point when minorities began expressing their desire for equality. Additionally, a large segment of the younger generation was eager to take a greater role in society, due in part to Kennedy's inspiring words and energetic persona. Philosopher Frithjof Benjamin of the University of Michigan recalled that "Kennedy created a climate of high idealism—it was evangelical. It was marvelous that we could make a beautiful world, a more compassionate world."[4]

Kennedy called for all Americans to take part in the country's destiny. He created the Peace Corps, an organization in which volunteers traveled to other lands to aid citizens in improving their communities. He called for Americans to travel to the moon, and he sought to ease tensions with the Soviet Union, a communist empire that used political and military means to expand its influence. The United States attempted to stop the spread of communism and protect free nations, and the struggle between the two countries was known as the Cold War. The fear of a destructive conflict

The presidential election of John F. Kennedy symbolized a new beginning for a new generation.

The Baby Boom

The relief of economic pressures for a large portion of the American population after World War II led to a sharp rise in the number of married couples having children. People call this period the "baby boom," and children born during that time have been nicknamed "Boomers." Historian Terry H. Anderson explains the size and scope of the baby boom:

> The enormous postwar birth rate lasted eighteen years, from 1946 to 1964, and it resulted in the largest generation in our history, over 70 million. ... Their sheer numbers changed the face of the nation. In 1960 ... there were only 16 million youths, 18- to 24-year-olds. The baby boom, however, brought about a dramatic shift. By 1970, the number of youth soared to about 25 million. Suddenly, the nation was young. The "sixties generation" included baby boomers who were born in the late 1940s and early 1950s, and the generation also comprised older siblings, those born during World War II. ... Consequently the sixties generation could be defined to include anyone who turned eighteen during the era from 1960 to 1972. The oldest was born in 1942 and turned 30 in 1972, and the youngest was born in 1954 and turned 18 in 1972. This generation numbered over 45 million ...

Terry H. Anderson, *The Movement and the Sixties: Protest in America from Greensboro to Wounded Knee.* New York: Oxford University Press, 1995, p. 89.

that could destroy both America and the Soviet Union was ever present in the minds of many people.

Not all of America's youth were enamored of President Kennedy. Tom Hayden, a student at the University of Michigan and a writer for *The Michigan Daily*, the school newspaper, wrote in 1960 that Kennedy was fascinating, but he was "an ambivalent character. ... There is a serious discrepancy in Kennedy between what he says and what he does."[5] For Hayden and many other politically active college students, Kennedy was ultimately a politician, and politicians could be practical, but they were frequently untrustworthy. People who held this view had other sources of inspiration beyond Kennedy, and it was in these artists and outcasts that the younger generation found its voice.

Ideas for a New Age

Beat writers such as Jack Kerouac and Allen Ginsberg challenged the predominant American culture in both their work

Sociologist C. Wright Mills helped shape the views of the new generation through his critiques of the social, economic, and political structure of American society.

their songs communicated concern for their fellow men and women and a yearning for freedom and peace. Bob Dylan, a twenty-year-old college dropout, moved to New York City in 1961 to make it big in music and visit his idol, folk music icon Woodie Guthrie. Dylan was inspired by Guthrie's work and also by the poetry of Allen Ginsberg, who introduced Dylan to other artists in New York.

Dylan performed in many venues in Greenwich Village, the downtown area of New York famous as a gathering place of artists and writers. Other popular performers included Joan Baez, and Peter, Paul and Mary, but Dylan stood out. Historian Allen J. Matusow writes, "Immersing himself in the left-liberal-civil-rights ethos permeating the Village in the early 1960s, Dylan wrote folk songs as protest. … He used figurative language and elusive imagery to distill the political mood of his time and place."[6] His popularity grew dramatically, and his music played an important role in the lives of young listeners.

In literature few books of the time captured the insanity of war and bureaucracy like Joseph Heller's 1961 novel *Catch-22*. Set in World War II, the story had a sincere antiwar message and followed the adventures of Captain Yossarian as he tried to obtain a discharge from the Army and go home. He wanted to plead insanity, but …

and their lifestyles, and they inspired young people to seek out views that were different than those passed down by their parents. The music and the literature of the late 1950s and the early 1960s contained a number of works that offered fresh and candid perspectives of American society and of people's place in America and in the world at large.

Music always played a role in capturing the spirit of the times in America, and it was no different in the early Sixties. Young singers and songwriters became part of the emerging folk music scene, and

There was only one catch and that was Catch-22, which specified that a concern for one's safety in the face of dangers … was the process of a rational mind. [Fellow pilot] Orr was crazy and could be grounded. All he had to do was ask; and as soon as he did, he was no longer crazy and would have to fly more missions. Orr would be crazy to fly more missions and sane if he didn't, but if he was sane he had to fly them.[7]

After the book became a critical success, the phrase "Catch-22" entered the American lexicon to describe any situation in which people find themselves presented with the illusion of choices but are prevented from making any real choice because the options are undesirable or unattainable.

Writers also addressed the issue of freedom of choice and people's place in modern society. Scholarly writers such as William H. Whyte, a sociology professor at Hunter College in New York City, explored the choices men made in the corporate world in his 1956 book, *The Organization Man*. He maintained that men, who dominated the office workforce during this period, frequently surrendered their individuality to succeed in the intricate and uncompromising corporate world. He also believed that men preferred the structured corporate atmosphere to the risky and independent life of the entrepreneur. "The urge to be a technician, a collaborator, shows most markedly in the kind of jobs [college] seniors prefer. They want to work for someone else. ... The relationship is to be for keeps. ... The odds favor the man who joins big business," Whyte concluded.[8]

Whyte's book supported the increasingly popular view among the young that corporations were stifling the freedom of individuals. The younger generation also pointed to other examples of how corporations were harming society. Marine biologist Rachel Carson's widely read 1962 book *Silent Spring* exposed the role of corporations in environmental pollution. Carson explained in detail the unseen damage pesticides and manufactured chemicals were causing to aquatic environments, the soil, and the air. She appealed for manufacturers to mend their ways, noting, "The rapidity of change and the speed with which new situations are created follow the impetuous and heedless pace of man rather than the deliberate pace of nature."[9]

All these writers and artists played a role in shaping the views of the new generation, but sociologist C. Wright Mills was perhaps the most influential. His writings frequently analyzed and criticized the economic, political, and social structure of American society. His 1956 book, *The Power Elite*, stated that America was ruled by what was commonly referred to as "the Establishment," a group of politicians, military leaders, and corporate executives who essentially made the decisions that guided the nation and determined its policy goals and direction. "[T]he people are of necessity confused and must, like trusting children, place all the new world of foreign policy and strategy and executive action in the hands of experts. ... others do not really care anyway, and besides, they do not want to know."[10]

Mills's view starkly contrasted with the image of a democratically elected government that American children had grown up with since the birth of the republic. As a scholar, his work as well as the work of Whyte, Carson, and others influenced university students on campuses around the country.

Joan Baez

Joan Chandos Baez was born on January 9, 1941, in Staten Island, New York. She developed an interest in music and a deep concern for human suffering at an early age. Her dedication to civil rights and the antiwar movement and her prolific songwriting and performing made her an integral part of the Sixties counterculture. She was present during many of the pivotal events of the decade.

Writer Arthur Levy explains Baez's impact on music:

Her earliest recordings fed a host of traditional ballads into the rock vernacular, before she un-selfconsciously introduced Bob Dylan to the world in 1963 and focused awareness on song-writers ranging from Woody Guthrie, Dylan, Phil Ochs, Richard Farina, and Tim Hardin, to Kris Kristofferson and Mickey Newbury, to Dar Williams, Richard Shindell, Steve Earle, and many more.

Songwriter Joan Baez's dedication to the antiwar movement and civil rights made her a vital part of the Sixties' counterculture.

She recorded her first solo LP for Vanguard Records in the summer of 1960, the beginning of a prolific 14-album, 12-year association with the label. Her earliest records, with their mix of traditional ballads and blues, lullabies, Carter Family songs, Weavers and Woody Guthrie songs, cowboy tunes, ethnic folk staples of American and non-American vintage, and much more—won strong followings in the U.S. and abroad.

"Joan Baez: Biography," Joan Baez Web site. http://www.joanbaez.com/officialbio08.html.

Seeds of a New Student Movement

The ideas that became popular on the college campuses in the early Sixties shaped a political movement known as the "New Left." Leftists embraced socialist ideals, such as government management of the economic and social structure of society through the redistribution of wealth. The traditional or old left in the earlier decades of the twentieth century focused on labor issues such as fair wages and workplace safety. The old left's association with communism, however, led to their downfall when the United States entered into the Cold War with the Soviet Union after World War II. They lost all credibility with the public, and they faded into obscurity. As a result, the younger leftists of the Sixties believed the old left no longer had anything to offer.

The college students who made up the New Left were often from affluent, educated, and politically liberal families. Many were encouraged by their parents to be free thinkers, and these students expressed guilt at the life of privilege they enjoyed compared to minorities and the poor. They were upset by the lack of equality blacks suffered in America, they were unsettled by the uneven distribution of wealth, and they feared that the Cold War would lead to nuclear annihilation. These students and the professors they trusted believed that the Establishment as defined by Mills was to blame for all of this. They decided the time had come to change it.

Among these students were Robert Alan "Al" Haber and Tom Hayden of the University of Michigan. In 1960 Haber, Hayden, and several others formed Students for a Democratic Society (SDS). This organization, with Haber as its first president and Hayden as field secretary, dedicated itself to fighting for civil rights and free speech, alleviating poverty, and challenging military institutions. They planned and took part in protests to raise awareness of these issues and to change laws and attitudes that perpetuated them. Over the next two years, SDS slowly grew to include chapters at colleges and universities around the country.

SDS held a national convention on June 11–15, 1962, in Port Huron, Michigan, where the leadership created a document to encapsulate their views and develop a structure for carrying them out. *The Port Huron Statement*, which was approximately fifty pages long, was the result of several days and nights of marathon debates and writing sessions. Constructed largely by Hayden, the *Statement*, as noted by historian Terry H. Anderson, "condemned the loneliness, isolation, 'emptiness of life,' the 'powerlessness of ordinary people.'"[11]

The *Statement* called for fundamental change in society to break the cycle of anti-democratic tendencies that SDS believed had pervaded America. It called for a national participatory democracy, which meant a decentralized government, in which everyone had the opportunity to express his or her views and that accommodated all opinions. SDS itself was set up in this fashion. There

The HUAC Protest: The Shape of Things to Come

Established in 1938, the House Un-American Activities Committee (HUAC) investigated and exposed anti-American groups and their activities. During the Cold War they focused their attention on real and suspected communists, but their investigative methods and the manner in which they dealt with witnesses had ruined the reputation of HUAC by the late 1950s. The Committee was the object of widespread criticism and ridicule, yet it continued to pursue its mandate despite growing opposition in Congress and in public.

On May 13, 1960, HUAC held a meeting at San Francisco's City Hall to investigate members of the University of California, Berkeley, faculty for supposed communist involvement. Berkeley students and supporters came to protest the hearing. Todd Gitlin, author of *The Sixties: Years of Hope, Days of Rage*, describes what happened next.

> … another body of upstarts insisted on their right to attend the hearings. … Kept outside of the hearing room, the demonstrators, most of them students, sat down in the rotunda and started to sing "We Shall Not Be Moved," a song of the Thirties. The police attacked them with high-pressure fire hoses, clubbed them, and hurled them down the marble steps …

> HUAC tried to link the demonstrators' actions to communist agitation, but their claims were largely unheeded, and the hearings closed down. A judge later dismissed charges against the demonstrators who were arrested that day.

Todd Gitlin, *The Sixties: Years of Hope, Days of Rage*. New York: Bantam Books, 1993, p. 82.

was no governing national body, and all of the chapters, though linked by common cause, were free to act of their own accord.

The *Statement* concluded by recognizing the university as the point of greatest influence in its push for change. "[T]he university is located in a permanent position of social influence. Its educational function makes it indispensable and automatically makes it a crucial institution in the formation of social attitudes."[12] SDS planned to use the university to reach the community beyond and establish a link to political power.

After Port Huron, SDS chapters sprouted up in many more universities. As their first major project, the organization established the Economic Research and Action Project (ERAP). SDS members in several northern cities worked to educate and empower poor residents to strive for better conditions in housing, social services, and the workplace. They made some progress, but overall ERAP achieved little. The inability to manage the government bureaucracy led many SDS members to believe that it was more worthwhile to confront the Establishment than to work within it.

Some SDS members questioned the efforts of ERAP, but virtually all of them recognized the value of taking part in the civil rights movement in the South. Participatory democracy, demonstrations, and the recognition of equal rights that were discussed in page after page of the *Port Huron Statement* were being acted out by Reverend Martin Luther King Jr. James Farmer, and many others. It was proof of SDS's views in action, so they were motivated to take part.

The Struggle for Racial Equality

Blacks in America were treated as second-class citizens despite the Constitution's guarantee of equal protection under the law. Circumstances were particularly bleak in the South. Institutionalized racism and segregation took the form of regulations known as Jim Crow laws that prevented blacks from holding decent jobs, receiving decent wages, and receiving the same social treatment as whites. Throughout the 1950s King and other activists spoke out against segregation and held mass demonstrations that emboldened young blacks coming of age in the Sixties.

On February 1, 1960, four black students went to the lunch counter at Woolworth's in Greensboro, North Carolina, and sat in the whites-only section. They were well dressed and polite, but the waitress refused to serve them because of their skin color. They returned the next day with more black students and received the same treatment.

Word of the event spread and sit-ins began in other segregated establishments in Greensboro and other southern cities. These actions were quite effective at drawing national attention. As sociologist Todd Gitlin writes in *The Sixties: Years of Hope, Days of Rage*, the demonstrators "threw the burden of disruption onto the upholders of white supremacy. Instead of saying that segregation ought to stop, they acted as if segregation no longer existed."[13]

The peaceful, non-violent resistance struck a nerve with the public in the North. Images of white locals harassing, humiliating, and beating blacks and white supporters while they marched or sat passively drew sympathy for the demonstrators. The more violent the reaction of racist whites, the more sympathy and support the civil rights cause drew.

The Freedom Rides of spring and summer 1961 brought a dramatic escalation of violence against the civil rights movement. Buses of blacks and whites traveled from the North to segregated cities in the South with the intention of performing sit-ins at illegally segregated bus terminals. Angry mobs met them in South Carolina and Alabama. Many were severally beaten, and one bus was set on fire. The local police did nothing

Sit-ins, like the one pictured at Brown's Basement Luncheonette in Oklahoma in 1958, drew national attention to the civil rights cause—equality of the races.

Dr. Martin Luther King, Jr. delivered his now infamous "I have a dream" speech outside the Lincoln Memorial in 1963. King recognized that the civil rights movement needed public attention in order to progress.

to stop the violence and made no arrests. Activist James Farmer, who organized the rides, turned to President Kennedy for help.

The civil rights leaders had grown disappointed with the Kennedy administration's lack of support for their cause. Foreign policy matters and strained relations with the Soviets had consumed Kennedy's attention. He supported civil rights, but he preferred to demonstrate a united nation to the world during tense times. He also did not want to lose political support in the South during this time. He instructed his brother and closest confidant, Attorney General Robert Kennedy, to tell Farmer and the riders to cool off. Farmer responded, "We have been cooling off for 350 years. If we cool off any more, we will be in a deep freeze."[14]

Kennedy did provide support, however, when James Meredith was denied admission to the University of Mississippi in the fall of 1962. Attorney General Kennedy personally took charge of the case, and Meredith was registered on September 30, but a riot broke out after it became known that Ole Miss had accepted its first black student. The National Guard was called out and peace was restored, but the larger struggle continued.

Centuries of racist policies were extremely difficult to overturn, and a divergence of opinion about how to combat them emerged within the civil rights movement. Young blacks had grown tired of their circumstances and wanted change. Their parents and older generations urged caution. They saw their lives, though far from equal to whites, as better than in earlier times. They feared that too much pushing against the white establishment could jeopardize the gains that had been made. King and other activists thought differently.

King was a keen observer of human nature, and he knew what it took to draw public attention. He also recognized that without that attention, the civil rights movement would drone on and make no progress. He targeted the segregated city of Birmingham, Alabama, in April 1963, for a series of demonstrations, fully realizing that Birmingham's public safety commissioner Eugene "Bull" Connor would strike back at the demonstrators in the violent, racist fashion that had helped the movement in the past.

Connor's methods of combating the demonstrators included nightstick-swinging cops, attack dogs, and high-pressure fire hoses. The images of black men and women, young and old, being beaten and bloodied outraged many around the nation. The events in Birmingham sparked demonstrations across the South, and white and black marchers traveled there to show support. The city plunged into chaos. Fires raged, jails overflowed, and economic collapse appeared imminent. The president and the attorney general called Birmingham officials and business leaders, and they agreed to integrate public facilities in the city.

President Kennedy addressed the nation on June 11. He called upon Congress to enact civil rights legislation, noting, "This Nation ... was founded on the principle that all men are created equal, and that the rights of every man are diminished when the rights of one man are threatened."[15]

Kennedy's announcement excited King and other civil rights leaders, but it angered racists. Just hours after Kennedy's speech, Medgar Evers, a field secretary with the National Association for the Advancement of Colored People (NAACP) was shot and killed outside his home by Byron De La Beckwith, a member of the Ku Klux Klan. De La Beckwith was arrested for the crime, but two all-white juries deadlocked without convicting him. In 1994 he was eventually retried and convicted of Evers's murder.

King, A. Philip Randolph, James Farmer, and other civil rights leaders spent much of the summer of 1963 organizing what became known as the March on Washington for Jobs and Freedom. The purpose of the march was a demand for meaningful civil rights legislation, an end to segregation, protection against police brutality, and public-works support for jobs and social services. Kennedy initially did not support the march because he feared it might derail the tenuous legislative negotiations already taking place in Congress. King and the others were undeterred, and Kennedy eventually gave his blessing.

There was concern that few would show up for the event, and there was the possibility that it could turn violent, but these concerns turned out to be unfounded. On August 28, 1963, 250,000 people showed up at the National Mall; 50,000 of them were white. The event was peaceful and drew international attention. Bob Dylan, Joan Baez, Peter, Paul and Mary, and several other musicians performed at the Lincoln Memorial. Many speakers addressed the crowd that day, but King's words were the most memorable. It wasn't the first time that he delivered his "I have a dream" speech, but this was certainly the largest crowd that ever heard it.

One particular line in the speech defined not only the entire gathering but also the civil rights movement as a whole. "I have a dream," King said, "that my four little children will one day live in a nation where they will not be judged by the color of their skin but by the content of their character."[16]

The immediate impact of the march was uncertain. It offered hope for change in the way blacks were treated in America, but little changed in the short term. Civil rights legislation in Congress remained stalled due to the tactics of a solid block of Southern representatives resistant to desegregation. Integration

had come to several southern cities and towns, but the advances were small in comparison to the injustices that many blacks still suffered. There was still much work to be done if meaningful change was going to take place.

The Erosion of Trust

The young Americans who had begun the Sixties dedicated to making a difference, took heart with the achievements of the civil rights movement and the work they were doing on university campuses, but progress was slow. Some of them admitted surprise at how entrenched the Establishment had become, and though they felt they could not completely trust Kennedy, he was one of their best hopes to facilitate change. Matusow writes, "Legions would follow Kennedy not because he was extraordinary but because he might be—not for his achievements but for his promise."[17] When Kennedy was assassinated on November 22, 1963, in Dallas, Texas, the trust American youth had for the older generation rapidly disintegrated.

Lee Harvey Oswald, a twenty-four-year-old former Marine and admitted communist, was arrested and charged with Kennedy's killing. When he was shot and killed during a prison transfer two days later, speculation developed about a conspiracy. Rather than suspecting the Soviet Union of being behind the crime, many young people drew the conclusion that Kennedy had been murdered by the Establishment because of his support for civil rights and for going further than any president in breaking down social barriers. According to this view, Oswald's murder was an effort to cover up the truth. Subsequent investigations ultimately supported the theory that Oswald had acted alone, but questions persist to this day.

Regardless of the motive for Kennedy's killing or who committed it, the act itself jarred the country. The images of the assassination, Vice President Lyndon Johnson taking the oath of office next to Kennedy's stunned wife Jacqueline, and Kennedy's state funeral played out before a grieving nation. The nation's youth and minorities were particularly affected. If a man like the president of the United States could be killed, what other acts of violence could be perpetrated in America? Now the new generation that Kennedy spoke of in his inaugural address was on its own. From this point forward they would be guided only by their own beliefs and instincts.

Chapter Two

Raising the Stakes

For the young and for disenfranchised minorities, the loss of John Kennedy in 1963 was a significant setback to their dreams of achieving peace and equality. There were no other leaders in Congress or elsewhere who they could believe in. In their view the Washington Establishment could not be trusted because they were perpetuating the racist and corporate policies of segregation and materialism the New Left had pledged to change.

Kennedy's successor Lyndon Johnson promised to continue the slain president's policies of racial equality and better international relations, and he injected an ambitious domestic program of his own into the agenda. The Great Society was a large package of legislative endeavors meant to provide health care, education, jobs, and social services to the nation's poorer classes. In his memoirs Johnson depicted the Great Society as an extension of the Bill of Rights. "But in our time a broadened concept of freedom requires that every American have the right to a healthy body, a full education, a decent home, and the opportunity to develop to the best of his talents."[18]

Though Johnson's openly liberal views seemed to match that of the *Port Huron Statement*, ironically the New Left trusted him less than Kennedy. In their view Johnson was a product of the Establishment. He had been a Washington politician virtually all his adult life. He was also a child of the South, and he had attended Southwest Texas State Teachers College, which was quite different from the prestigious northern universities that were the home of the New Left. Additionally, in August 1964 Congress gave Johnson almost unanimous support to extend America's military commitment in South Vietnam after North Vietnamese patrol boats reportedly fired on U.S. ships in the Gulf of Tonkin. America had been sending material support to

The Beatles

Rock and Roll music became increasingly important to the generation of the 1960s as the years progressed, because it reflected their desire to break free of the values and views of their parents. The music influenced the young, and the young in turn influenced the music. At the same time, the music itself was changing, and one band in particular, influenced by jazz, blues, and 1950s pop, took rock & roll in a direction that shaped not only the music of those who followed them, but the fashion, politics, and culture of the 1960s and beyond.

The British band The Beatles helped shape the culture, politics and fashion of the Sixties, as well as the music of those that followed them.

The British band The Beatles made their first public appearance in America on the popular "Ed Sullivan Show" on February 6, 1964, and the mostly young audience went absolutely wild. Many of the live shows the Beatles later performed inspired similar reactions. Their press agent Derek Taylor witnessed their power over the crowd:

> I have never seen anything like it. Nor heard any noise to approximate the ceaseless, frantic, hysterical scream which met the Beatles when they took the stage after what seemed a hundred years of earlier acts. All very good, all marking time, because no one had come for anything other than the Beatles ...

> Then the theatre went wild. First aid men and police—men in the stalls, women mainly in the balcony—taut and anxious, patrolled the aisles, one to every three rows.

> Many girls fainted. Thirty were gently carried out, protesting in their hysteria, forlorn and wretched in an unrequited love for four lads who might have lived next door.

"The Beatles History: Introduction," The Beatles. http://www.thebeatles.com/#/history/Introduction.

Vietnam for years to prevent a communist insurgency from toppling a sovereign government, but now American troops were fighting full-scale battles in the tiny jungle nation.

The protests and the demonstrations seemed to be leading nowhere. War had become more, not less, likely. Civil rights marchers were still being hit with nightsticks and fire hoses. The youth went beyond disappointment. They had become thoroughly distrustful, angered, and motivated to take matters into their own hands. They turned their back on society in greater numbers, developing their own plans, their own goals, and their own culture.

Pushing the Artistic Envelope

Art, literature, music, and theater took a bold turn in the mid-Sixties by reflecting a greater desire among youth to find a voice for their distinct views. Older generations frequently criticized these new forms of artistic expression as simplistic or even obscene, but the young countered that adults simply didn't understand. By the conventional standards that had defined art up to the 1950s, it was difficult to imagine, for instance, that an artist such as Andy Warhol could become rich and famous by painting Campbell's Soup cans and Brillo boxes. The older generation thought of landscapes, portraits, and sculpture when they thought of art, not consumer products.

Warhol was born in Pittsburgh, Pennsylvania, on August 6, 1928, and he gained work as a talented commercial illustrator in New York during the fifties. He began working in a relatively new form of art known as Pop, which consisted of visual representations of familiar items and icons of the popular culture. Warhol's first New York exhibit opened on November 6, 1962, and featured canvases in which representations of Marilyn Monroe, Campbell's Soup cans, Coca-Cola bottles, and 100-dollar bills were repeated over and over again, symbolizing what Warhol viewed as the machine-like repetition that existed in American culture. The exhibit was a sensation, and Warhol began experimenting in other media including film and music.

Many of Warhol's films were not meant for commercial release and often focused on some of the more mundane elements of everyday life. One film featured a man sleeping for several hours, and another featured someone eating a banana. Others were strictly adult in their imagery and subject matter. All of Warhol's artistic endeavors invariably explored life and the human condition. Photographer John Coplans, in referring to specific Warhol paintings, explained, "Warhol is open to everything.... His work is literal throughout: those are Campbell's soup cans, that is an atomic explosion, here is a car crash, and the accident that can happen to anyone."[19]

Warhol's fame transcended the art world, and his studio, the Factory, was the scene of many gatherings that featured famous musicians and actors as well as young acolytes eager to be in his next movie. Young artists admired

Many young artists of the Sixties admired Pop artist Andy Warhol because he proved that anything could be considered art.

Warhol because his work was proof of their view that everything was art. Traditional artists criticized this idea because it meant that art could be created without any true inspiration or discipline. As historian William L. O'Neill writes, "When everything becomes potentially a work of art, and everyman an artist, anyone could claim to be living for truth or beauty without having to prove it."[20] The power of art to communicate ideas would be lost.

Enclaves of artists gathered in other areas of the country outside of New York. Near San Francisco such a group formed around author Ken Kesey. Kesey, born on September 17, 1935, worked briefly in a California state mental hospital, which would become the inspiration for his 1962 anti-establishment novel, *One Flew Over the Cuckoo's Nest.* While at the hospital Kesey volunteered to be a subject for psychological drug experiments, which included LSD, a powerful synthetic that induces hallucinations and alters sensory perceptions. Kesey praised the drug and invited a group of people to join him in taking LSD, popularly known as acid, and exploring new states of psychological consciousness. They collectively became known as the Merry Pranksters.

Kesey's home was the scene of numerous parties that featured strobe lights, an elaborate sound system, and other elements designed to enhance acid trips, a term used to describe the time period during which a person was under the influence of LSD. Todd Gitlin explains that, in the summer of 1964, "a dozen

Pranksters careened around the country in a beat-up-Day-Glo-painted super-stereo'd bus named FURTHER, gobbling and smoking vast quantities of drugs, freaking out local citizens…having a high old time."[21] The adventure was chronicled in Tom Wolfe's 1968 book, *The Electric Kool-Aid Acid Test,* and it added to the popularity of the Pranksters among California's growing youth scene.

Prankster parties became larger and more elaborate, and they showcased live rock bands that were becoming popular in San Francisco through 1964 and 1965. The San Francisco music scene included Jefferson Airplane, Iron Butterfly, Quicksilver Messenger Service, the Grateful Dead, and other groups who were experimenting with surreal lyrics, long guitar solos, and musical improvisation. They rapidly gained popularity among the younger generation across the country, and their style of music became known as acid rock because it often served as the perfect soundtrack to an acid trip. Their style of clothing—colorful, layered patchworks—and their unconventional lifestyles simultaneously reflected and inspired the changes that were taking place in the youth culture in cities around America.

Theater was similarly affected by the changes taking place in other arts. O'Neill writes, "The cult of youth romanticism, the preference for instinct and spontaneity, the urge to propagandize flourished."[22] Theater groups were established in New York, San Francisco, Los Angeles, and elsewhere that offered entertainment much different than the escapist musicals or conventional dramas of Broadway. They engaged in improvisation and audience participation, and presented plays that scrutinized the Establishment and opened up to ridicule virtually any view not embraced by the younger generation. Some of these plays contained nudity, and many of them used foul language, elements of theater virtually unheard of in the Sixties. In some cases, communities protested to shut down such productions, but these theater groups still developed a small and dedicated following.

Comedian Lenny Bruce drew a great deal of negative attention during this period because of his choice of subject matter and his use of foul language. Born in New York on October 13, 1925, Bruce worked as a writer and performer in the 1950s, making a name for himself on the comedy circuit. He frequently tackled subjects such as religion, politics, morality, law, drugs, and his own Jewish heritage. Among his signature lines were: "In the Halls of Justice the only justice is in the halls," and "The liberals can understand everything but people who don't understand them."[23]

The Merry Pranksters, a group of people exploring the effects of LSD led by Ken Kesey, drove around the country in a Day-Glo painted bus, consuming vast amounts of drugs.

The Underground Press

The Free Speech Movement and the emerging counterculture inspired numerous self-published newsletters and magazines that featured fiction, poetry, and writings on music and the arts, philosophy, and politics. Historian Terry H. Anderson explains:

"There is a credibility gap between the press and the people," declared a former journalist for the United Press International and the *New York Times*, John Wilcock, "because the newspaper owners are plain and simple liars. ... As a result, the Hippies just don't read the national papers." Wilcock began publishing Other Scenes while thousands of freaks and activists developed three national underground wire services and over 600 papers which eventually had a circulation of about 5 million. High school kids printed up some 3000 randomly printed tracts, while older siblings created a library of posters, leaflets, and newsletters. ... The message was Us versus Them, and the publishers knew what side they wanted to be on. Most never pretended to be accurate or to publish "All the News That's Fit to Print." Underground reporters were gonzo journalists; that is, they participated in the event and then wrote the article from their perspective.

Terry H. Anderson, *The Movement and the Sixties: Protest in America From Greensboro to Wounded Knee.* New York: Oxford University Press, 1995, p. 245.

Bruce was arrested for obscenity on October 4, 1961, after swearing onstage. He was acquitted, but law enforcement monitored many of his performances afterward. Bruce was in and out of court several times over the next several years, and a growing drug habit did not help his fortunes. Many cities banned him from performing because of his material, and nightclub owners refused to book him for fear of being arrested. On August 3, 1966, Bruce was found dead of an apparent morphine overdose.

Bruce's fans, including many younger audiences, considered his controversial work groundbreaking and thought provoking. They interpreted his death as brought on by the Establishment's censorship of his ideas. Still, others besides Bruce were willing to take up the battles for free speech.

A Wave of Student Activism

At the opening of the fall 1964 semester, several student activists at the University of California, Berkeley, set up tables on campus to promote various student

Students of the University of California protesting the arrest of Jack Weinberg in 1964. Weinberg defied a political activity ban, which encouraged the crowd to enact their rights to free speech.

political organizations, many of them with leftist tendencies. The university had strict rules against such political activity, and they ordered the tables removed and called for disciplinary action against the students who defied the ban. On October 1, student Jack Weinberg deliberately set up a table for the Congress of Racial Equality (CORE) in defiance of the ban. He was promptly arrested, but when he was placed in a police car to be taken away, hundreds of students surrounded the car and prevented it from leaving. Weinberg sat in the car for thirty-two hours (minus bathroom breaks) while students took turns standing on its roof and encouraging the crowd to claim their right to free speech. Among them was Mario Savio, a well-spoken philosophy major who had volunteered in the civil rights movement. The standoff ended when the university agreed to drop charges against Weinberg.

Weinberg's willingness to face arrest and the spontaneous actions of the students to defy the police was a completely new experience on a college campus. "The students' basic demand is a demand to be heard, to be considered," Weinberg remarked of the demonstration, "to be taken into account when decisions concerning their education and their life in the university community are being made."[24]

The event kicked off what became known as the Free Speech Movement at Berkeley. Throughout the fall semester, students continued to rally to the cause. Weinberg and several others organized demonstrations and sit-ins on campus, but Savio became the unofficial spokesman for the movement due to his oratorical skills. "Last summer I went to Mississippi to join the struggle there for civil rights," Savio said at the time. "This fall I am engaged in another phase of the same struggle, this time in Berkeley. ... the privileged minority manipulates the university bureaucracy to suppress the students' political expression."[25]

Several students involved in the events of October 1 were charged with inciting a riot, and on December 2 approximately one thousand students took over Sproul Hall, the administration building on campus. Throughout the night the students congregated in "freedom classes," open discussions, and sing-alongs led by Joan Baez. The students ignored pleas by university administrators to leave the building, and at 3:30 A.M., police entered and arrested more than eight hundred demonstrators.

By this point the movement had grown beyond the issue of political expression on campus. The list of demands that students presented during their demonstrations included a repeal of *in loco parentis* (in place of parent) regulations that, among other things, restricted relations with members of the opposite sex, set dormitory curfews, and banned alcohol consumption. It seemed hypocritical to students that they be governed in this way when people their age who did not go to college were not subject to such laws.

Savio and the others also expressed resentment at the influence of corporations on campus. It was not uncommon for major corporations to offer grants to universities, nor was it unusual for them to conduct interviews with graduating students who were prospective employees; after all, most young people went to college to obtain better paying jobs. Savio equated the university and its corporate sponsors as a machine and the students as raw materials with little say in their own lives. He said, "There is a time when the operation of the machine becomes so odious ... that you can't take part ... and you've got to put your bodies upon the gears ... and upon all the apparatus and you've got to make it stop."[26]

News of the events at Berkeley spread to other campuses, and soon protests were taking place at the University of Michigan, Syracuse University, Ohio State, and several other schools. By early

Benjamin Spock

In 1946 pediatrician Benjamin Spock published *The Common Sense Book of Baby and Child Care*, a manual for new parents about how to take care of their newborns and infants. The book was revolutionary because it encouraged a more flexible attitude toward child rearing than in earlier generations. It became one of the best-selling books of all time, and influenced how the baby boom generation was raised. Historian Steve Gillon explains:

> Spock rejected his own upbringing, which emphasized strict feeding schedules and unchanging routines, and insisted that parents respond to the needs and schedules of their children. "Trust yourself, you know more than you think you do," he reassured worried new parents. His ideas reflected the optimism of the age, reinforcing that personality was malleable if only parents developed the right skills. … Whether they purchased the book, as one [in] five mothers did, borrowed it from their local library, read the excerpts in magazines and newspapers, or listened to him on television, Boomer mothers found it impossible to escape Spock's influence.
>
> Although Spock emerged as an outspoken liberal activist during the 1960s, the ideals he espoused had more of a cultural than a political impact on the Baby Boom generation. The emphasis on individual psychology and the discovery of "inner" happiness produced a generation consumed with self-fulfillment.

Steve Gillon, *Boomer Nation: The Largest and Richest Generation Ever and How it Changes America*. New York: Free Press, 2004, p. 11.

1965 the students who had taken part in the Free Speech Movement began protesting America's growing involvement in Vietnam. A bombing campaign in North Vietnam in February motivated a demonstration led by SDS at the Oakland Army Terminal, which was a departure point for troops headed for Southeast Asia. It was one of the first significant off-campus antiwar protests.

Savio remarked of the growing movement, "The bigger the machine we'd built, the greater the problems that it seemed to unearth."[27] There were plenty of students to tackle these problems. The first baby boomers began college in the fall 1964 semester, and university enrollment across the country rose 37 percent. Two million boomers attended college in 1964. By 1970 there were 8 million.

The Sisterhood Steps Up

One problem that had been unearthed, though not necessarily by the student movement, was the issue of women's place in America. It had been widely assumed for generations that women were most satisfied in the role of wife and mother, and advertising, television and film, books, and magazines reinforced this view. This view was so pervasive that some medical professionals believed that women who insisted on having careers ran the risk of wrecking their marriage or raising children who would become social or sexual deviants.

Many women in otherwise happy marriages were not satisfied with their lives as the popular culture at the time suggested. They wanted more out of life than cooking, cleaning, and sending the kids off to school. Writer Betty Friedan recognized this and called it "the problem with no name." Her 1963 book, *The Feminine Mystique*, drew on numerous

Betty Friedan's book, The Feminine Mystique, *concluded that societal views kept women from achieving their full potential.*

interviews with women and came to the conclusion that entrenched societal views were keeping them from achieving their full potential.

"For the first time in their history," Friedan wrote, "women are becoming aware of an identity crisis in their own lives … [that] will not end until they … turn an unknown corner and make of themselves and their lives the new image that so many women now so desperately need."[28] Friedan encouraged women to find work that was fulfilling and could help them to establish their identity. Her book became required reading for the emerging feminist movement, a movement she helped advance when she cofounded the National Organization for Women (NOW) in 1966. NOW was dedicated to creating better job opportunities, better wages, and fostering independence of thought and action among women.

Young women in SDS and the student movement also sought more respect for their roles. It seemed odd that within a movement that sought racial equality and free speech, women would be treated as subordinate to men, but that was the case in the early Sixties. In 1964 women made up half the SDS membership, yet only 6 percent held leadership roles. The rest typed, cleaned offices, and fetched coffee. One young female activist noted, "They had all this empathy for the Vietnamese, and for black Americans, but they didn't have much empathy for the women in their lives."[29]

Activists Mary King and Casey Hayden wrote a memorandum examining the subordinate role of women in society and suggested that the movement they worked in could offer an opportunity for bringing about gender equality. "The very fact that the country can't face, much less deal with, the questions we're raising means that the movement is one place to look for some relief."[30] The argument made sense to many women in the movement, but the civil rights battle loomed larger for SDS and the entire student movement.

The Battle for Civil Rights Intensifies

Noticeable similarities existed between the student movements on campus and the civil rights movement in the South. Members of both the student the civil rights movements shared similar goals and relied on similar tactics. Savio, Weinberg, and many others who spurred the Free Speech Movement had spent time in the South in 1964, and they had seen firsthand the power of direct action.

Direct action in the civil rights movement produced a significant victory when President Johnson signed into law the Civil Rights Act of 1964 on July 2 after several months of intense congressional debate. The law banned racial discrimination in public places and privately run establishments such as restaurants, theaters, and hotels. It also gave the attorney general power to file suit against anybody who discriminated on the basis of race, and the government could pull funding for any institution that did the same. Notably absent from the law was a guarantee of voting rights for blacks.

Johnson recalled in his memoirs, however that "there was no time to rest. Tensions in the South were still running high."[31] The continued resistance to integration in the Deep South heightened these tensions. Racist whites were aggravated by the influx of white and black volunteers from the North who sought to register local blacks to vote and open schools for poor black children. Freedom Summer, as this period in 1964 came to be known by activists, was a dangerous time. Members of the Ku Klux Klan attacked local blacks who cooperated with the volunteers. Two northern white volunteers and a young black civil rights worker disappeared on June 21 near Philadelphia, Mississippi, and were feared murdered. Their bodies were found on August 4.

The activists were not deterred by the murders, but they did express disdain for Johnson, who had refused to provide protection for the volunteers. The president, motivated by political concerns, did not want to further upset southern Democrats in the months leading up to the presidential election by ordering federal troops into their districts.

Conflict in the Civil Rights Movement

Growing dissension was occurring within the civil rights movement as well. The beatings, intimidation, and murders led a growing number of blacks to question the viability of the non-violent methods of Martin Luther King. One particular critic was Malcolm X, a Muslim minister who believed that violence against blacks should be met with violence. He urged blacks to take pride in themselves and rely on one another, not whites, to improve their lives.

Malcolm X was born Malcolm Little on May 19, 1925. His father died at the hands of the Klan for his civil rights work when Malcolm was thirteen. Malcolm's early life was one of petty crime, and it earned him an eight-year prison sentence. While in jail Malcolm became a member of the Nation of Islam, commonly referred to at the time as the "Black Muslims." This organization preached self-reliance among blacks through a regimented lifestyle that included celibacy outside of marriage and banned tobacco, pork, and alcohol. Black Muslims also believed that blacks were the original people of the earth and that whites were devils who used deceit to take over the world.

Malcolm became a powerful speaker, second only to the Nation's leader, Elijah Muhammad. Malcolm drew a number of young black men in the northern ghettos to the organization, which grew to 25,000 members in 1963. He called for a complete separation from whites, stating that after hundreds of years of oppression, blacks could only achieve a decent life by turning their backs on white America. This philosophy came to be known as "black nationalism." Malcolm also criticized King's civil rights work and called him a chimp for believing that blacks could achieve their goals by working with whites. Malcolm labeled the August 1963 March on Washington a farce and said the demonstration was "run by whites in front of a statue of a president who has been dead

Malcolm X, who established the philosophy of Black Nationalism, visits Temple 7—a Halal restaurant patronized by black Muslims.

for a hundred years and who didn't like us when he was alive."[32]

Relations between Malcolm and Muhammad became strained after Malcolm referred to Kennedy's assassination as "chickens coming home to roost."[33] Tensions were further complicated by the revelation that Muhammad had fathered children with other women outside his marriage. Malcolm announced his break from Nation of Islam on March 8, 1964. He established the Organization of Afro-American Unity and made a pilgrimage to Mecca.

After his return Malcolm tempered his speeches to include words that were less inflammatory and more inspirational. He received numerous death threats, presumably from the black Muslims, but he continued his work unabated. On February 21, 1965, while giving a speech, Malcolm X was shot to death by three men in Harlem. His funeral drew hundreds of people, and all members of the civil rights movement mourned his death, even though Malcolm had criticized many of them during his life.

Violence on American Streets

King continued his own brand of nonviolent demonstrations, and, with other civil rights activists, organized a march

After police arrested a young black driver, rioting erupted in Watts, a neighborhood in Los Angeles, California.

from Selma to Montgomery, Alabama, in the struggle for black voting rights in that state. On Sunday, March 7, 1965, approximately six hundred marchers got as far as the Edmund Pettis Bridge in Selma before Sheriff Jim Clark and his police force intercepted them. As historian James T. Patterson describes, Clark's men mercilessly attacked the marchers: "Charging with rebel yells...[they] swung bullwhips and rubber tubing wrapped in barbed wire. More demonstrators fell back,

seventy of whom were later hospitalized."[34] The event became known as "Bloody Sunday."

Subsequent marches drew more public attention, and on March 24, the crowd reached the outskirts of Montgomery. A direct result of the event was the passage of the Voting Rights Act on August 6 that banned discriminatory practices, such as poll taxes and literacy tests. The celebration of this victory was short-lived.

On August 11, 1965, a California Highway Patrolman pulled over a drunk driver in an African American neighborhood near the Watts district of Los Angeles. The young black driver resisted arrest. When the police subdued him, a crowd of onlookers became hostile, sparking a serious confrontation with the officers. Tensions rapidly escalated over the next several hours. Passing white motorists were pulled from their cars and beaten. Stores were looted and burned, and the entire area plunged into chaos.

Police and 13,900 national guardsmen restored order after six days. Property damage was estimated at $35 million, and hundreds of buildings had been burned or looted. There was no conclusive estimate as to the number of rioters, but the most reliable put the crowd at 30,000. More than 1,000 were injured, and 34 were killed.

Watts was not the first riot in America's urban ghetto, but its scope, size, and duration indicated that recent federal legislation had not eased racial tensions. It also indicated that the plight of blacks was not confined to the South. The economic situation was bleak all over the country. In most major cities blacks had almost double the unemployment rate of whites. On average, blacks made 60 percent of what whites did, and they worked more often at menial jobs that offered no opportunity for advancement.

These unsettling economic realities were a cause of the Watts riot and of a growing current of cynicism within the civil rights movement. Voting rights did not change the fact that African Americans lived in poverty. It didn't matter if blacks could sit in the same section of a theater or a restaurant as whites; most of them could not afford to patronize such establishments. Furthermore, a long-standing tradition of racism made blacks feel completely unwanted in white America. The question on many young black minds was reflected by writer James Baldwin, "Do I really want to be integrated into a burning house?"[35]

Chapter Three

Turning On, Tuning In, Dropping Out

Just as the events of the mid-Sixties led young blacks to contemplate giving up the dream of an integrated society, young whites were also reevaluating their position in society. The real economic issues behind African American poverty were not being addressed. The government program that was designed to alleviate this problem, President Johnson's Great Society program, was being financially picked apart to fund America's growing involvement in Vietnam. And the widening antiwar movement had no effect on the escalation as American troop strength in Vietnam rose from 23,000 in 1964 to 385,000 in 1966. Casualties also rose dramatically, from 206 American deaths in 1964 to more than 6,000 in 1966 alone.

SDS and other New Left groups took up the argument that America was instigating the conflict, not the communist North Vietnamese. They rejected the position that America was preventing another attempt at international communist expansion like several others that had taken place since 1945. Older Americans who supported the war questioned the patriotism of the young. The young, in turn, questioned the humanity of their elders for waging war on a sovereign nation.

The war was but one of many topics where a generation gap developed. University administration and government allocation of social services were others. Sociologist Todd Gitlin explains: "The young insisted that their life situation was unprecedented (and therefore they had no one to follow); the older, that they *did* understand, so well, and with so many years' advantage, that they knew better (and therefore should be followed)."[36]

Many young people began to question whether they should make an effort to liberalize a society that seemed closed to their ideas. Those who decided not to

Cesar Chavez

Cesar Estrada Chavez was born on March 31, 1927 near Yuma, Arizona. His parents ran a small grocery store, but lost everything in the Great Depression. They were forced into the hard life of migrant laborers and toiled on California farms with large numbers of Mexican immigrants. Chavez grew up motivated to achieve a better life for himself and his community. He became active in voter registration drives for Mexican Americans, and he also supported movements for better working conditions and higher wages for farm workers.

This excerpt from *Cesar Chavez: A Brief Biography with Documents* provides more detail:

Caesar Chavez supported movements for better working conditions and led the Delano Grape Strike.

… Chavez organized the National Farm Workers Association in 1962 (also known as the Farm Workers Association [FWA]). In the next two years, Chavez's possibilities of success seemed especially slim because so few workers were rallying to his cause….Chavez labored tirelessly, meeting with workers and their families, compiling lists of prospective members for the organization, and encouraging farm families experiencing financial and health problems…. By 1964, his new FWA had enrolled more than a thousand members …

In 1965 the Delano area of California, one of the richest producers of grapes in the state, was run by businesses that ran their farms like fiefdoms, treating the workers horribly and paying them little. Chavez led a strike, though the FWA was ill prepared for a long struggle. Chavez's union eventually won the strike, and he became a national hero in the struggle for civil and employment rights.

Chavez died on April 23, 1993. His birthday is celebrated as a holiday in several states, and many parks, schools, and cultural centers have been named in his honor.

Richard W. Etulain, ed., *Cesar Chavez: A Brief Biography with Documents.* New York: Palgrave, 2002, p. 8.

simply walked away and developed their own society. At this point a true alternative culture, or counterculture, developed. Youth in America had already embraced a number of social components—art, music, politics, gender, and racial relations—that challenged the mainstream of American culture. Within the counterculture, everything from clothing and hairstyles to views about sex, drugs, and religion was markedly different from the mainstream.

Haight-Ashbury

The Haight-Ashbury district of San Francisco, also known as Hashbury or the Haight, was the unofficial capital of the counterculture in the Sixties. The district was in economic decline through much of the 1950s, and middle-class families left in large numbers for the suburbs. Members of the counterculture, predominantly college dropouts and hippies, replaced them, flocking to the area in large numbers to take advantage of the cheap rooms and vacant homes. By the mid-Sixties, hippies were everywhere in the Haight.

Hippie was the term applied to anyone who had essentially rejected the conventional culture and lived life on his or her own terms. Hippies rejected capitalism and seldom held jobs except when it was absolutely necessary to obtain basic needs such as food and shelter. They believed in nonviolence, love, and community, and they often congregated in groups called "communes," in which responsibilities, possessions, and sometimes even sexual partners were shared. They maintained a relaxed view of life, and they did not trouble themselves with planning for the future. They lived in the moment.

Hippies were also easily recognizable for their long hair and their patchwork or vintage clothing, although being a hippie wasn't so much about the visual representation as it was about the state of mind. One university student stated at the time, "The hippie movement is not a beard, it is not a weird, colorful costume, it is not marijuana. The hippie

As the Sixties' counterculture reached its peak, people danced, smoked marijuana, and wore colorful outfits, becoming part of the Summer of Love.

movement … is a philosophy, a way of life, and a hippie is one who believes in this."[37]

One group that actively promoted the hippie worldview was the Diggers. Named after seventeenth-century English revolutionaries, the Diggers were a troupe of actors who engaged in street theater and created spontaneous art and social gatherings known as "happenings." According to their Web site, they "were the progenitors of many new (or newly discovered) ideas such as … the first Free Medical Clinic … tie-dyed clothing, and communal celebrations of natural planetary events, such as the Solstices and Equinoxes."[38] The Diggers handed out free clothing, food, and drugs, such as marijuana and LSD, at happenings and in Golden Gate Park, where hippies often congregated. They operated out of a storefront they called the Free Frame of Reference, where people could also obtain these items.

The fact that they handed out drugs free of charge demonstrates how common drug use was in Haight-Ashbury and how prevalent drugs were in the counterculture. The counterculture considered marijuana and LSD tools by which to explore the self and develop a sense of community with others, namely people who were also using drugs. Marijuana use was so common that people often smoked it in public in such permissive areas as the Haight or Greenwich Village.

LSD, which was virtually unknown to the public before the 1960s, grew rapidly in popularity, thanks in large part to Timothy Leary. Leary, a psychologist at Harvard University, began experimenting with LSD and other psychedelic drugs in 1960. He believed that LSD could treat alcoholism, reform convicted criminals, and expand a person's consciousness. His experiments drew negative attention at Harvard due to his own habitual use of the drug and his experiments with undergraduate students. The university fired Leary in 1963, but he continued his experiments and became a spokesperson for the drug.

The federal government outlawed LSD in 1966. Its widespread use had led to a number of highly publicized "bad trips," or psychological episodes that brought on emotional problems in habitual or unstable users. The drug itself did not cause physical health problems, but there was always a possibility that people under its influence could be a danger to themselves or others. Frequent use could also lead to a mental breakdown in which the user had trouble distinguishing reality from fantasy even when not under the drug's influence.

None of this stopped Leary. He believed that his teachings could prevent these negative side effects. He established the League for Spiritual Discovery in 1966 and became a self-professed guru of LSD. An LSD cult of sorts formed around him, and he readily took up the role. He grew his hair long, wore flowing white robes, and embraced elements of Buddhism and Eastern mysticism, which had become a fad within the counterculture.

Leary made an appearance in the Haight on January 14, 1967, for the Human Be-In, a happening that was organized in Golden Gate Park. The event drew 20,000 people, and Leary encouraged the crowd to "Turn on to the scene, tune in to what is happening, and drop out—of high school, college, grad school, junior executive—and follow me the hard way."[39] Acid rock bands performed, and Allen Ginsberg recited Buddhist chants to bless the gathering.

Due to his experiments with the drug, psychologist Timothy Leary contributed to the rapid growth of LSD popularity in the Sixties.

People wore colorful costumes, smoked marijuana, burned incense, and danced.

By the summer of 1967, the counterculture's impact in America had reached its peak. Popularly known as the Summer of Love, it was during this period that young people around the country adopted the style of dress and music that was common in the Haight. The district

Monterey Pop

The Monterey International Pop Festival of June 16–18, 1967, was the first major rock music festival in America, and it drew a total of 200,000 spectators. Taking place in the central California community of Monterey, the festival was a major event during the Summer of Love. The musicians who performed represented some of the most popular acts of the time—Simon and Garfunkel, the Animals, Jefferson Airplane, Janis Joplin, the Who, the Mamas and Papas, and twenty-six other groups. One image that will be forever linked with the festival is the image of guitarist Jimi Hendrix lighting his guitar on fire during his performance.

Reporter John Bassett McCleary recalls the festival:

The Monterey International Pop Festival … was not just a musical event. It was not just an excuse for young people to come together to do frivolous, youthful things. It was the beginning of a new kind of gathering. It was the beginning of a new form of music. It was the beginning of a political and spiritual movement. Everyone who attended Monterey Pop was changed by the experience.

Monterey Pop was the convergence of music, psychedelics and Eastern sensibility. … Many things can be said about the uniqueness of Monterey Pop. We can say that everyone was beautiful. We can talk about the peace and love displayed by those who were there. We can tell of how the music moved us.

Hendrix played as if he were a god, yet mortal as all of us are. Country Joe became the most truthful politician we had ever heard…. And Janis Joplin cried for every woman and man, yet demanded that we stand up to the reasons for our tears.

John Bassett McCleary, "40 Years Ago." *Monterey County Herald*, http://www.montereyherald.com/pop-festival/ci_6107823?nclick_check=1.

itself became a beacon for hippies who wanted to be a part of the scene, but it also was a draw for teenage runaways and thrill seekers looking for nothing more than free drugs and wild parties. The communal atmosphere of the Haight began to disintegrate.

Drug trafficking became rampant as dealers moved in to take advantage of the scene for profit. Available housing dried up and rents soared. Law enforcement cracked down on drug trafficking and building code violations. The influx of close to 100,000 people into San Francisco had put a severe strain on public resources and caused a sharp rise in crime. Allen J. Matusow writes, "By the end of the year, *reported* crime in Haight-Ashbury included 17 murders, 100 rapes, and nearly 3,000 burglaries."[40] Some Diggers started carrying weapons for self-protection.

At the end of the summer, the scene and everything that was a part of it had played itself out. Virtually all of the new arrivals had left. The indigenous population had the district to themselves once again, and they celebrated it on October 6, with a mock funeral. The Death of Hippie included an empty coffin and a funeral procession through the Haight, and it signified that the hippie scene as it was known in San Francisco had come to an end.

Leaving American Society Behind

Those most dedicated to the hippie lifestyle left society altogether and formed rural communes. These communards, or commune residents, sought to create their own societies from the ground up. They grew their own food and built their own shelters. It was a life that required long hours and hard work, and it was reminiscent of the experiences of the settlers of the eighteenth and nineteenth centuries. They had few, if any, creature comforts such as electricity, running water, or appliances. Only the hardiest souls were able to stick it out for long. Those who joined communes for the novelty of

Many dedicated to the Hippie lifestyle left society to form communes—a lifestyle in which the practices were reminiscent of the settlers of the 18th and 19th centuries.

it or because they thought they could sit around and smoke dope all day quickly became discouraged.

Those who stayed were drawn to the freedom that the commune lifestyle afforded. No one made judgments about a person's background, sexuality, or style of dress. The only rules that existed—and there were few rules—were the ones the communards made themselves. As a result each commune had its own distinct structure. Some were based on religious ideals; others operated like artist colonies. Some had group marriages, but others encouraged monogamy. One constant among them was the lack of private possessions. Everything was shared equally; and any money was for the good of the group.

The communes experienced a varying degree of success. Those populated exclusively by people from urban areas tended not to last long, but those that survived eventually became self-sustaining. Communards developed crafts that could be sold to raise money. They rented space and sold food at co-ops when there was a surplus.

A whole category of literature developed in which communards around the country shared tips on growing food, cooking, and other subjects. One of the most popular magazines was the *Whole Earth Catalog*, which premiered in fall 1968. In its first issue, author Stewart Brand recognized a developing "power of the individual to conduct his own education, find his own inspiration, shape his own environment, and share his adventure with whoever is interested. Tools that aid this process are sought and promoted by the *Whole Earth Catalog*."[41]

Members of the counterculture who were dedicated activists thought that dropping out and joining a commune meant turning one's back on the New Left movement and the struggle to change society. That was the whole point for the hippies. In their view society was too violent and therefore doomed to destroy itself. They believed they no longer had any stake in it. Those who did vowed to fight on.

The Growing Antiwar Movement

The expansion of America's military in Vietnam aggravated the antiwar movement at home. In April 1965, SDS organized a march in Washington, D.C., and up to 25,000 people attended. The crowd far exceeded the organizers' expectations, and its size and scope also caught the attention of the national media. Public resistance to the draft also began with a demonstration in May at Berkeley, when a number of students burned their draft cards and carried a coffin to the local draft board office.

The government had resorted to drafting young men to meet the troop requirements in Vietnam that could not be met by active duty personnel and reservists. In the first half of the Sixties, draft calls averaged about 100,000 per year, with fewer than 200 evasions, or failures to report by draftees, for each of those years. In 1965 the number of draft calls doubled, and in 1966 calls

The expansion of military in Vietnam fueled the antiwar movement at home. Many demonstrations took place, like the burning of draft cards on the Pentagon's steps.

went up to 380,000. At this point the number of evasions rose dramatically. More than 200,000 young men evaded the draft during the war, but only about 3,000 ever went to jail for their crimes.

Draftees had a variety of deferments to legally avoid the draft, such as getting married, attending college, or having a medical condition that prevented military service. In some cases young men claimed trumped-up medical or psychological issues to avoid combat. In extreme cases some fled to Canada or Mexico. Student deferments in particular were a source of social tension because the poor who could not afford college had a disproportionately higher chance of being selected for combat.

Burning one's draft card was an entirely symbolic antiwar gesture. It did not by any means alleviate a young man's duty to show up for military induction if his number was called. Furthermore, if that man was a student, he was deferred in any case and, therefore, had nothing to worry about. Congress was outraged by such protests, and, on August 31 with almost unanimous support, the government passed legislation that made it illegal to destroy draft cards. The $10,000 fine and possible jail time did not deter activists, and the card burnings continued.

The protests also became larger and more frequent. On November 27, 40,000 protesters marched to the White House, then to the Washington Monument. On March 26, 1966, 20,000 protesters held a rally in New York City. Many more events large and small were held in cities across the country. International protests also took place, with 4,000 young people descending on the U.S. Embassy in London on July 3, 1966.

SDS membership grew dramatically because of its leadership role in these demonstrations. It began drawing from a larger pool of college students who previously had expressed no opinion on the war, but who were now motivated by fear of the draft and what they perceived as the hypocrisy of the war. They wondered how it was possible for the government to guarantee freedom for the peasants of Vietnam when it could not guarantee freedom for blacks in America. They also did not fear the spread of communist expansion in a poor agricultural country ten thousand miles away.

SDS's leadership debated whether to rededicate the organization entirely to the antiwar effort. In keeping with their original charter as a decentralized organization, they voted against the idea because it meant that individual SDS chapters would lose the freedom to choose their own causes. As one SDS leader, Paul Booth recalled, "We really screwed up. We had the opportunity to ... make SDS *the* organizational vehicle of the anti-war movement.... Instead, we chose to go off in all kinds of different directions."[42]

Another development affected SDS and its ability to be a viable leader in the movement. Time had changed much of the leadership of the organization and the antiwar movement in general. Many of the students who had started with the organization in 1962 had graduated and moved on with their lives. The younger students who were getting involved in 1966 and 1967 were more radical and less patient than their predecessors. One SDS leader, Carl Davidson, advocated a new strategy of "disruption, dislocation, and destruction of the military's access to the manpower, intelligence, or resources of our universities."[43]

SDS and other antiwar groups lived up to these bold words during Stop the Draft Week in late October 1967. Vigorous protests unfolded across the nation at Selective Service centers, ROTC offices on college campuses, and against corporate recruiters with defense contracts. The week closed with a massive march in Washington that ended at the steps of the Pentagon on October 21. Approximately 100,000 people took part, and the event led to a vigil that went on into the night. Some protesters treated the event as a happening and took part in chants they claimed would levitate the Pentagon. Soldiers and police officers engaged some of the more unruly demonstrators and made more than six hundred arrests, among them writer Norman Mailer, who detailed

The San Francisco Mime Troupe

Artistic expression was a major element of the Sixties counterculture, and numerous theater groups and artists' communities were established. Their work often challenged conventional society and parodied politics and popular culture. One of the most well known groups of the decade was the San Francisco Mime Troupe. The Troupe's Web site explains their origins:

The San Francisco Mime Troupe, founded as an experimental project, was one of the most popular groups of artistic expression in the Sixties' counterculture.

R.G. Davis, trained as a dancer and mime, founded the company soon to become the San Francisco Mime Troupe as an experimental project of the now-legendary Actors' Workshop in 1959. The ensemble's first pieces were silent—not pantomime, but movement "Events" with visual art elements and music.

In 1961, Davis began exploring a spoken, but still movement-based, form: *commedia dell'arte*: the popular theater of the Italian Renaissance, played by stock characters in masks. In 1962, he took a commedia play, THE DOWRY, outdoors for a single performance in San Francisco's Washington Square Park, passing the hat afterwards.

The following year, the city's Recreation and Park Commission denied the Troupe a permit to perform on grounds of "obscenity." The ensuing court case, argued by [California attorney] Marvin Stender, established the right of artists to perform uncensored in the city's parks.

The San Francisco Mime Troupe celebrated its fiftieth anniversary in 2009.

"San Francisco Mime Troupe History," San Francisco Mime Troupe. http://www.sfmt.org/company/history.php

the events of the Pentagon protest in his book, *The Armies of the Night*.

Young Americans Outside the Counterculture

The large antiwar demonstrations and the hippie gatherings of 1967 were not representative of the majority of the American public. These events received widespread media coverage, but polling conducted at that time indicated that a majority of Americans, including people under thirty, actually supported the war effort.

It is a misconception to believe that all of America's youth in the 1960s were against the war, or that they were all part of the counterculture. The Sixties experienced the largest college and university population in history to that time, and this population made up a significant portion of the antiwar movement, but it was a much smaller portion of the nation's youth. The U.S. Census bureau notes that in 1967, for example, of the 20 million Americans ages eighteen to twenty-four, only 25 percent were enrolled in college. Some youths not in college supported the antiwar movement or considered themselves part of the counterculture, but many more did not.

Professor Paul Lyons refers to these youths as "'the silent majority baby boomers,' that is, those of the Sixties generation, mostly white and middle American, who seemed to go about their business—school, dating, sports, marriage, work, kids, insurance payments ..."[44] The view of these youths reflected that of their elders in that they did not see a counterculture so much as they saw a group of spoiled, unappreciative children of privilege. They maintained that the protesters rejected college educations and high-paying jobs, then flaunted that rejection in front of a nation in which a majority of people could not attain what they had so brazenly cast aside. Regardless of the merits of this position, it was clear that not only was there a noticeable divide between young and old but also among the young themselves.

One organization that served as a focal point for youths who held conservative views was Young Americans for Freedom (YAF). YAF was founded in 1960, and, in September of that year, its leadership gathered in Sharon, Connecticut, at the estate of conservative writer and editor William F. Buckley Jr. to outline the organization's principles. The one-page *Sharon Statement* became the guiding document of YAF. Historian John Andrew writes that the central principles of the *Statement* included "the idea that liberty was 'indivisible' and that political freedom would not 'long exist without economic freedom.' Government had only three functions: 'the preservation of internal order, the provision of national defense and the administration of justice.'"[45]

YAF grew rapidly. The organization held a rally at Madison Square Garden in 1962 that drew 18,000 people. By 1965 it claimed 20,000 members in 250 chapters across the country, making it larger than SDS. Members of YAF were not protesters by nature. Instead, they communicated

Those outside of the counterculture movement, like writer William F. Buckley, Jr. (center), believed counterculture youth rebelled simply to upset their elders.

their views through articles in various publications, including their own flagship magazine, *New Guard*. They supported candidates for public office who shared their free-market, anti-communist ideals. They also supported the reasons for fighting the Vietnam War, although they came to disagree with the way the Johnson administration was conducting it.

YAF members also shared a growing concern in Middle America about the disintegration of traditional values in society. Counterculture behaviors, such as casual drug use, free love, foul language, and a general contempt for authority, validated this concern. In YAF's view the counterculture youth was rebelling against these values only to upset their elders. As one baby boomer recalled, "I never could tell where my husband's sideburns ended and his moustache began, but he didn't care as long as it irritated his mother."[46]

Dedicated members of the counterculture disagreed with YAF and their elders as to the reasons behind their behavior, but they freely admitted a disdain for authority and the Establishment that exercised it. They also admitted that their protests and peace marches were not achieving the desired effect of diminishing the Establishment. More direct action was necessary.

Chapter Four

From Protest to Resistance

The antiwar and civil rights movements in the closing months of 1967 became more confrontational as a radical view took hold among protesters. SDS demonstrators in Oakland, California, and New York City threw rocks and bottles at police. In the ghettos, blacks were also becoming more militant. Near simultaneous riots in Newark, New Jersey, and Detroit, left dozens dead, thousands injured, and cost billions of dollars in property damage. Protest had given way to resistance. Todd Gitlin writes, "Fighting back could be defended, arguably, as part of a strategy for ending the war, since neither civil disobedience nor Establishment grumbling seemed sufficient by itself."[47]

Resistance to the Vietnam War grew steadily as 1967 gave way to 1968. The American death toll from the conflict reached almost 20,000, and victory appeared no closer than it had in 1964.

President Johnson's popularity was at an all-time low, but he insisted that the country was winning in Southeast Asia. On January 30, 1968, the North Vietnamese communists launched the Tet Offensive, a nationwide onslaught of 80,000 troops that attacked numerous American positions. The offensive was beaten back in a matter of weeks, and the North Vietnamese lost almost their entire invasion force, but the battle was a severe blow to American morale. In Washington and around the country, many people who had previously supported the war wondered how it was possible for North Vietnam to launch such a massive attack if America was supposedly winning the war.

Johnson faced two formidable challenges within his own Democratic Party when the presidential primary season began in March. Minnesota Senator Eugene McCarthy ran on a pledge to end the war, and he came within three hundred votes

American soldiers walk up a hill in Vietnam. The Vietnam War caused many radical and confrontational antiwar protests back home.

of beating the incumbent Johnson. Shortly after that New York Senator Robert Kennedy declared his candidacy for president. Johnson announced on March 31, that he would not seek reelection, and he also called for a bombing halt in North Vietnam to jumpstart peace talks.

The war continued to rage, however, and so did the movement against it.

Enter the Radicals

The National Student Association, a collection of college and university student governments in the 1950s and 1960s, conducted a survey of campus unrest in 1968. The survey determined that 221 major demonstrations occurred between January 1 and June 15, involving close to 40,000 students on 101 different campuses.

The young activists of the New Left who had formed SDS and led the free speech movement at Berkeley earlier in the decade were no longer leading these demonstrations against the war. A group of younger students known as radicals were taking control of the movement. Radicals differed from the earlier members of the New Left in that they were not interested in making changes in society. Participatory democracy and peaceful demonstrations were a waste of time in their view. They wanted to destroy the Establishment. Carl Davidson rationalized this goal by pointing out that the current social order was "totalitarian, manipulative, repressive, and anti-democratic ... without legitimacy in our eyes, they are without rights."[48]

This revolutionary ideal inspired bolder and more aggressive moves against authority. The most prominent concern was that it would lead to widespread violence. Another concern was that the radicals were seeking power for its own sake. They did not plan ahead. They only knew what they were fighting against, and they had only a vague idea of what they wanted to replace and what they were targeting for destruction. They were also

Jim Morrison: A Portrait of Counterculture Excess

The Doors were a rock music group that came together in Venice Beach, California, in 1966. Their first single, "Light My Fire," reached number one on the Billboard charts, and they rapidly became one of the biggest draws in rock. Front man Jim Morrison became a legend not only for his dark and mysterious lyrics, but his iconic stage persona and his excessive lifestyle. Many members of the counterculture embraced him for these reasons.

Shortly after the Doors reached stardom, Morrison's drinking grew out of control. He became unruly in the studio, on stage, and in public. As noted in the *Rolling Stone Illustrated History of Rock and Roll*:

> Morrison began to flirt with new and more dangerous forms of exhibitionism. Creating havoc on planes, getting arrested in airports. Pushing his way to the stage of the Troubadour and raving drunkenly. Onstage at a Doors concert in New Haven, telling the crowd how he and a girl were maced by police in the dressing room; stage suddenly covered with police, the whole thing stupid.

> On March 1, 1969, Morrison was arrested for indecent exposure during a concert in Miami. The group maintained a loyal following, but their days of live performance with Morrison were over. In March 1971 Morrison moved to Paris, presumably to escape the limelight and focus on his poetry. Unfortunately, he continued his hard lifestyle, and died of respiratory failure on July 3, 1971. He was twenty-seven years old.

Anthony DeCurtis and James Henke, *Rolling Stone Illustrated History of Rock and Roll*. New York: Random House, 1992, p. 390.

not interested in seeking common ground. Berkeley activist Michael Rossman was asked at one point by a local councilman, "If we give in to your present demands, will this satisfy you, or is this only one in a long list of demands?" Rossman responded, "Don't worry, we'll always be one demand ahead of you."[49]

Columbia: A University Under Siege

The bold attitudes of the radicals found a home at Columbia University in New York City, an Ivy League school with a prestigious reputation. In March 1967 the school's SDS chapter discovered that research was being conducted on campus for the Institute for Defense Analysis (IDA), a non-profit policy organization involved in national security matters of a scientific and technical nature. This instigated antiwar protesters who wanted to remove all vestiges of government and military ties to the university system.

At the same time SDS joined blacks from the adjacent community of Harlem in protesting the university's construction

In protest of building a new gymnasium, Columbia students lined the ledge outside the office of university president Grayson Kirk. Columbia revealed a new level of intensification in the battle against the Establishment.

of a gymnasium in a nearby park. Local residents had fought against the project for years, arguing that the university had improperly appropriated the land. Columbia offered to set aside a portion of the completed structure, which was built into the side of a hill, as a community center for the people of Harlem. When locals learned that the center would be on the lower level of the gym, they accused the university of practicing segregation, and the project became known locally as Gym Crow.

The convergence of the antiwar and student rights movements on the Columbia campus energized Mark Rudd, who was elected president of SDS in April 1968. Rudd, born November 17, 1954, claimed to have been a leftist all of his young life. Just a month before his election as SDS chapter president, he had taken a trip to Cuba, professed his love and admiration for its dictator Fidel Castro, and met with North Vietnamese communist representatives. Returning to America, Rudd was eager to begin his revolutionary work.

On April 23, 450 people from Rudd's SDS and Columbia's Student Afro Society (SAS) marched on Hamilton Hall, an office and classroom building. They seized the building and held a dean hostage for twenty-four hours. Local black militants arrived later that evening, and SAS asked SDS to vacate the premises, then proclaimed Hamilton Hall to be renamed Malcolm X Hall. SDS then stormed into Low Library, which also housed administration offices, including the offices of university president Grayson Kirk.

A thousand students sympathetic to the protest took over three more buildings in the next few days. Rudd set himself up in Kirk's office, smoked his cigars, and rifled through his files. Along with his colleagues, he announced SDS and SAS's demands to the administration. Historian Stewart Burns writes that "the crux of the demands … was to stop Gym Crow, sever all ties with the IDA, and grant amnesty to the occupiers."[50]

Outside the buildings, the campus was pitched into chaos. The media descended on Columbia to report on the event, classes were disrupted, and protests for and against the occupation took place. Many students did not support the seizure of the buildings, and a group of athletes and fraternity brothers formed a blockade around Low Library to keep supplies from reaching its occupiers for three days.

Negotiations between the administration and SDS proved useless. SDS would not entertain compromise on any issue, and the administration refused to grant amnesty to the occupiers. On April 30, New York police stormed all the occupied buildings except Malcolm X Hall, from which the SAS and local militants left peaceably of their own accord. More than 700 white protesters were arrested, and 150 were injured during the scuffle with police. Columbia ultimately scrapped the gymnasium project and broke ties with the IDA, but thirty students were suspended from campus for their role in the occupation.

Columbia represented a new level of escalation in the youth movement's battle against the Establishment. The protests against the war and the battle for civil rights and student rights were now all part of a larger recognized movement driven by radicals to seize power and bring down the Establishment by any means necessary. Tom Hayden, who was present at the occupation, wrote, "The goal written on the university walls was 'Create two, three, many Columbias'…. It meant expand the strike so that the U.S. must either change or send its troops to occupy American campuses. At this point the goal seems realistic."[51]

World Protesters Find Common Cause

In several nations around the world, the younger generation had become as vocal, as angry, and as committed to change as the youth in America, in some cases more so. Anti–Vietnam War protests took place in several cities across Western Europe. These nations had largely refused to take part in the war effort, but

In response to Alexander Dubček's attempts to reform the Marxist system, 200,000 Soviet troops invaded Czechoslovakia to remove Dubček and his supporters from power.

because they were America's allies, protesters interpreted their relationship as unspoken support for U.S. actions in Vietnam. Other reasons for protest were similar to those in the United States—student rights, an end to real or perceived government repression, and an end to the militaristic stance that had perpetuated the cold war.

In France, demonstrations against the country's education and employment systems led to a series of student strikes that prompted the government to close the Sorbonne University in Paris and several other schools. As recorded in an eyewitness diary entry from May 6, "Layers upon layers of new people were soon drawn into the struggle. The student union and the union representing university teaching staff called for an unlimited strike. For a week the students held their ground, in ever bigger and more militant street demonstrations."[52] Clashes with baton-wielding police left hundreds injured and drew broad sympathy from the population. A general strike of students and two-thirds of the French workforce brought the country to a standstill. President Charles de Gaulle dissolved the national assembly and called for new elections in June, after which point the strikes came to an end, and order was restored.

In West Berlin during this same period, students demonstrated against the conservative university system and a floundering economy. The police responded harshly and inflamed the passions of the demonstrators. The government debated passing a series of emergency acts that would suspend civil liberties, and in May 80,000 students and workers marched in the capital of Bonn to protest the measure. Despite the large showing, the emergency acts passed, and the student movement fell apart.

Student unrest was not confined to Western Europe. In Japan, students had been protesting against the country's security treaty with the United States, fearing it would lead to Japan being dragged into a U.S. war. Many students also opposed the Vietnam War because they felt the many U.S. military bases in Japan made them in some way responsible for its continuation. Throughout 1968 more than one hundred protests took place at universities around the country, with one particularly violent clash happening at Tokyo University while students marked the one-year anniversary of the death of a fellow protester. More than 140 students were arrested, and 110 policemen were injured.

Protests also took place in Soviet dominated Eastern Europe, a region known as the communist bloc. In communist countries the government controlled the economy and all media. Freedom of speech was heavily restricted or simply nonexistent, and dissent was not tolerated. On January 5, 1968, reformer Alexander Dubček became the leader of the communist bloc country of Czechoslovakia. He immediately set about easing restrictions on public speech, and he enacted free market principles to ease the country's economic difficulties. Dubček's actions led to what became known as the Prague Spring. Cestmír Císar, a member Dubček's government who was responsible for abolishing censorship, recalled, "We wanted to overcome fear and create an open atmosphere. We just put into practice what the people were thinking."[53]

The Soviet Union disapproved of the reforms of the Prague Spring, fearing that other communist bloc countries would call for similar changes and loosen their control over the region. Leaders in Moscow urged Dubček to reverse his policies, but he stood firm. On August 21, 200,000 Soviet troops, joined by soldiers from the bloc countries of Bulgaria, Hungary, and Poland invaded Czechoslovakia. They seized control of the airport and confined Czech troops to their barracks. Tanks rolled through Prague, the capital city. The Soviet force gained control of the country in a short period of time, and 72 Czechs were killed. Another 266 were severely wounded. Dubček and his supporters in the government were removed from power. Several other supporters were jailed or executed for their role in the movement.

The heavy military response in Czechoslovakia appalled the governments of the West, and they publicly denounced the Soviet Union. Student protesters in Paris, West Berlin, Tokyo, and the United States were not as surprised by the brutal reaction of the communist ruling establishment. These young people had been demonstrating against their governments for years, and when they choked on tear gas, bandaged head wounds, and nursed broken bones, they became aware of what governments were capable of when power was threatened. Some of those in the United States who were now taking a more militant approach figured it was only a matter of time before the big guns of America's armed forces were turned against its own people.

Black Power

Blacks in the urban ghetto had already seen the U.S. military deployed in their neighborhoods. Civil unrest during the riots in Los Angeles, Detroit, and Newark was brought under control only after uniformed soldiers with automatic weapons patrolled the streets. A new militancy in the black community was growing in response.

One of the first black activists to embrace this militancy was Stokely Carmichael. Carmichael, born June 29, 1941, was a member of the Student Nonviolent Coordinating Committee (SNCC), a civil rights group that operated in the South during the early Sixties. On June 16, 1966, Carmichael was arrested while taking part in a civil rights march. Upon his release from jail, Carmichael addressed a rally. "This is the twenty-seventh time I have been arrested—and I ain't going to jail no more. … We been saying freedom for six years and we ain't got nothin'. What we gonna start saying now is Black Power."[54]

The phrase "black power" invigorated blacks and unsettled whites. There was much debate over whether Carmichael meant it as a term of empowerment or

The Black Panthers were founded in an attempt to instill pride in the African American race. The party crafted a list of demands that included an immediate end to police brutality, free health care, and decent housing for blacks.

aggression, but his subsequent actions indicated that both views were probably accurate. He became the leader of SNCC later in the year, and in December set about removing whites from the organization. Carmichael's reason for this was that, "Integration is a subterfuge [ploy] for the maintenance of white supremacy ... [that] reinforces among both black and white, the idea that 'white' is automatically better and 'black' is by definition inferior."[55]

Carmichael, like Malcolm X before him, reasoned that blacks needed to establish their own identity, and he became a proponent of Black Nationalism. This stance had the potential to instill pride in a race of people who had been treated as second-class citizens, but many blacks did not want to live in a separate world from whites; they wanted to live in the same world as equals. Consequently, the ejection of whites from SNCC marginalized its effectiveness. White financial support disintegrated, and moderate blacks left the organization in droves. Carmichael's black-power rhetoric also alienated many people. James T. Patterson notes, "By early 1968 SNCC was dying so fast that it was ridiculed as the 'Non-Student Violent Non-Coordinating Committee.'"[56]

The Black Panther Party for Self Defense filled the void left by SNCC's demise. Huey Newton, a twenty-four-year-old college dropout, and Bobby Seale, a twenty-nine-year-old activist, founded the Black Panthers in Oakland, California, on October 15, 1966. They crafted a ten-point program that amounted to a list of demands for the black community that included completely free health care, full employment, decent housing, education that explained the oppression of the black people, and an immediate end to police brutality. This last item was inspired by the Panthers' complete distrust of the police force, which they believed was racist. They exploited a little-known California law that permitted people to openly carry loaded firearms and began policing their own neighborhood with shotguns.

The image of black men wearing black berets and leather jackets, openly carrying shotguns on the streets of Los Angeles sent fear through much of white America. The radical white leftists of SDS and other organizations were enamored of the Panthers for their brazen challenge of the Establishment. The community-oriented actions of the Panthers, such as providing free breakfast and social services for needy blacks, was overshadowed by their openly confrontational behavior.

On May 2, 1967, Panthers stormed the California State Assembly to prevent passage of a law that would repeal the gun-carrying provision that was at the heart of their community policing program. The law passed, and the Panther patrols came to an end. The event drew national attention, and Black Panther chapters started up in other cities. The FBI and municipal law enforcement agencies began enhanced surveillance of the Panthers, and tensions grew significantly between Panthers and the law.

Newton got into a shootout with two police officers on October 28, 1967, and one officer was wounded and the other was killed. Newton was also wounded, and he claimed that in the chaos of the moment, the officers accidentally shot each other. The black and radical white community believed that the police were trying to assassinate Newton, and that, even if he had shot the officers, it was in self-defense. While Newton was in jail awaiting trial, an ex-convict named Eldridge Cleaver rose to prominence in the Panthers by establishing a "Free Huey" campaign. The New Left joined the campaign, but Newton was convicted of voluntary manslaughter in 1968.

Cleaver had written extensively about race issues when he was in prison, and he wanted to extend the political reach of the Panthers. He made a deal with Carmichael in late 1967 to absorb what was the left of the SNCC infrastructure and make Carmichael the Black Panther Prime Minister. Cleaver believed the union between Carmichael and the Panthers would allow blacks an opportunity to achieve real political power in America.

Rage Boils Over

Martin Luther King Jr. remained committed to peaceful means of achieving power for blacks in America, but in 1968 the actions of the Black Panthers and the

Racial Issues on Olympic Display

The 1968 Summer Olympic Games in Mexico City took place during a time of worldwide turbulence. The Vietnam War was claiming thousands of lives on both sides. Student protests raged in American and Europe, and people in Czechoslovakia faced down Soviet tanks in their fight against communist repression. America's racial divide had reached new heights after the murder of Martin Luther King Jr.

It was against this backdrop that U.S. Olympic track team members Tommie Smith and John Carlos competed in the 200-meter race. Smith won the gold medal and shattered the world record. Carlos won the bronze. When the two black men stood on the podium to accept their medals, they each raised one black-gloved fist into the air, a salute that had become synonymous with the black power movement in the United States.

The two men were expelled from the Olympics for overtly injecting politics into the apolitical forum. As Amy Bass notes, however, the impact of the moment may have been worth that price:

American track and field athletes Tommie Smith (center) and John Carlos (right) each raised a fist, signifying the Black Power salute. Their gesture created a moment of confrontation that denounced racism in the United States.

Despite the brilliant nature of the race itself, the symbolic medal ceremony that followed, of course, proved most historic. ... With their gesture, they created a moment of resistance and confrontation with dominant and existing forms of racial identity. ... In front of a global audience of approximately four hundred million people, the duo used their moment to denounce racism in the United States.

Amy Bass, *Not the Triumph but the Struggle*. Minneapolis: University of Minnesota Press, 2002 p. 239.

sporadic rioting in northern cities overshadowed his message. He refused to be swayed by militant blacks, and he urged his own supporters to continue their nonviolent campaign. He addressed a rally on April 3, 1968, in Memphis, Tennessee: "I want you to know tonight, that we, as a people, will get to the Promised Land. And I'm happy, tonight. I'm not worried about anything. I'm not fearing any man. Mine eyes have seen the glory of the coming of the Lord."[57]

On April 4, while standing on a balcony at his hotel, King was shot by James Earl Ray, a drifter and career criminal. News of the assassination spread quickly, and blacks and whites around the country expressed shock and dismay. Robert Kennedy, who was on the presidential campaign trail at the time, broke the news at a rally in Indianapolis that night. He urged people to remain calm out of respect for King's peaceful legacy, but it was already too late.

Over the next several days, riots and civil disturbances broke out in dozens of cities across America. In Chicago, demonstrators clashed with police, and 4 people were killed and 48 more were injured. In Los Angeles on April 6, Black Panthers Eldridge Cleaver and Bobby Hampton engaged in a shootout with police. Hampton was killed, and Cleaver was arrested for attempted murder. He later jumped bail and fled to Algeria.

Many of King's supporters gravitated toward Kennedy in the aftermath of the assassination, and his campaign gained momentum. Senator McCarthy had been the favorite of most mainstream democrats, but the younger Kennedy changed that. He was often equated to a rock star for drawing large crowds of young people who climbed over one another just to get within arm's reach of him.

Kennedy won the June 4 primary in California, securing a solid delegate lead for the upcoming Democratic National Convention. Moments after giving his victory speech, he was shot to death by Sirhan Sirhan, a mentally disturbed Palestinian who claimed to be motivated by Arab nationalism. The conspiracy theories that surrounded the death of Kennedy's brother in 1963 were revived, and once again the Establishment was blamed for his murder.

Kennedy's murder and the death of King just two months prior plunged the country into deep despair. The names of these two men were added to a growing list of killings in recent years that indicated that the heritage of peaceful American political discourse had been replaced by a wave of violence that could not be brought under control.

Chicago

The Democratic National Convention set for August 28 in Chicago would determine which candidate the party would choose to challenge Republican Richard Nixon for the presidency. Johnson's Vice President Hubert Humphrey seemed to be the logical choice, but McCarthy still commanded a great deal of support. The politics of the event, however, was overshadowed by what took place outside the convention hall.

The Chicago Seven (top row second from left is Tom Hayden, bottom left is Jerry Rubin, and bottom right is Abbie Hoffman) were radical protesters whom skillfully exploited media interest in the counterculture in order to communicate their message.

A group of radical protesters known as the Youth International Party, or Yippies, gathered in Chicago with the announced plan of disrupting the convention. The Yippies, formed by Abbot "Abbie" Hoffman, his wife Anita, Jerry Rubin, and others, were committed to revolutionary change in America, but they pursued their goals in a comical and theatrical fashion. They did not enjoy widespread support among the antiwar movement, however, because they were seen as irrational and needlessly provocative, which, of course, they freely admitted.

They skillfully exploited media interest in the counterculture to spread their message. "Get out of school, quit your job," Hoffman urged. "Come on out and help build the society you want. Stop trying to organize everybody but yourself. Begin to live your vision."[58] Hoffman and the other Yippies were eager to cause chaos. They spread rumors about their plans for the convention that included dumping LSD into the Chicago water supply, dressing up women as prostitutes to seduce convention delegates, and setting large lots of marijuana on fire to get the city high.

Yippie humor was lost on Mayor Richard Daley, who held an iron grip on Chicago politics and was in no mood for unrest while his city was on national display. He put 23,000 police and national guardsmen on duty with orders to stop the demonstrations. On the first night of the convention, when the 10,000 Yippies, hippies, and other assorted protesters refused to adhere to the 11:00 P.M. curfew in Lincoln Park, the police moved in to disperse them. At that point the battle was joined, and it continued throughout the convention.

The protesters were caught off guard by the sheer violence of the police. Officers, who removed their badges to avoid being identified, waded into the crowds swinging clubs and dispersing clouds of tear gas. Innocent bystanders were often caught in the chaos. Some police also attacked reporters to prevent them from communicating the event to the public, but that was a futile gesture. The beatings and the violence inflicted in Chicago played out before an international audience on television. It also deeply divided the Democrats in the convention hall, who eventually nominated Humphrey as tear gas drifted in through the air ducts.

Hoffman, Rubin, and five others were eventually charged with conspiracy to incite a riot. The subsequent trial became a farce in true Yippie style with the defendants, known as the Chicago Seven, engaging in speeches, pranks, and other antics that disrupted the proceedings. They were found guilty of inciting a riot, but the conviction was later overturned based on cultural biases and the presiding judge's antagonistic attitude toward the defense.

The aftermath of the Chicago convention marked a crisis point for the nation. The cultural divide widened. Daley was simultaneously vilified by the young and celebrated by the old for his actions. Writers and former activists Stewart and Judith Albert note, "A report for the National Commission on the Causes and Prevention of Violence concluded that a 'police riot' had taken place in Chicago between August 21–28, 1968."[59] Middle America believed the country was coming apart. Radicals believed this as well, but they were happy about it. America had entered a period of unrest unmatched since the civil war.

Chapter Five

The Counterculture Loses Its Way

The hope and promise embraced by the baby boomers at the beginning of the Sixties had mostly evaporated by 1969. The liberal politicians who ran the country for much of the decade, Lyndon Johnson chief among them, had failed completely in delivering on their promises of peace for the country, prosperity for the people, and equality for minorities. The Vietnam War claimed the lives of 17,000 Americans in 1968, nearly doubling the total number of deaths in the conflict. Spending for the war put a strain on the economy, and rising inflation and unemployment threatened to wipe out the gains made earlier in the decade.

President Richard Nixon began his term on January 20, 1969, with the promise of bringing the war to an end and uniting the country. He immediately set about reducing the number of American troops in Vietnam, but he covered America's exit from Southeast Asia with a massive bombing campaign into countries under North Vietnamese influence that had not previously been involved in the conflict. As a consequence, his words rang hollow with a growing antiwar movement supported by a broader segment of the younger generation.

The fact that more people were rallying to the antiwar cause should have been a boost for the New Left. The convergence of black militants, student activists, and even some everyday citizens demonstrated a perceptible desire for change, but that convergence was short-lived. The Black Panthers and SDS, the two most prominent leftist organizations, were being torn apart by internal political squabbles over the direction and tactics of their respective groups.

These arguments were often about minute details, and they were comparatively minor in the greater context of the movement, but they grew out of

The Manson Family

Charles Manson, born November 12, 1934, was a drifter and an aspiring musician who briefly drifted around the periphery of the San Francisco counterculture scene in 1967 and 1968. Dennis Wilson of the musical group the Beach Boys and others thought Manson and his "family" of hippies and social misfits were odd. What they did not know was that Manson was a deeply disturbed career criminal who had spent more than half of his life behind bars by the time he was thirty-two.

During his time in San Francisco, Manson had gathered a small following. Former Los Angeles County District Attorney Vincent Bugliosi explains:

Cult leader Charles Manson convinced several of his followers to commit brutal murders, including that of actress Sharon Tate, which could be blamed on the blacks.

[Manson's followers] were also young, naïve, eager to believe, and, perhaps even more important, belong. There were followers aplenty for any self-styled guru. It didn't take Manson long to sense this.

Manson claimed he foresaw the decline of the Haight even before it came to full flower. Saw police harassment, bad trips, heavy vibes, people ripping off one another and OD'ing in the streets. … He got an old school bus, loaded up his followers, and split …

Manson convinced his followers that a race war would destroy society and that they should strike first by committing a horrible crime that could be blamed on blacks. At his command several men and women brutally murdered seven people, including actress Sharon Tate, who was eight-months pregnant, in the Los Angeles area on August 9 and August 10, 1969. The perpetrators and Manson were later convicted of the crimes that had shocked the nation and symbolized the darkest elements of the counterculture.

Vincent Bugliosi and Curt Gentry, *Helter Skelter: The True Story of the Manson Murders*. New York: W.W. Norton, 1974, p. 225–226.

proportion for two reasons. The stubborn non-negotiable attitude that emboldened leftists when applied to the Establishment became a debating tactic that they frequently applied within their own organizations. No one was willing to back down, because everyone claimed to be right. Second, paranoia had set in and affected the judgment of group leaders. This paranoia was encapsulated in an article by draft resister Lenny Heller. "If you want to be a revolutionary, you have to be awake, you can't have one minute's peace, you're alive every single moment.… It is intense, and there are distortions that take place under that intensity."[60]

War in the Ghetto

The very nature of the revolutionary ideal that young leftists adopted meant that they were constantly looking over their shoulders, wondering if the Establishment was just around the corner. This was certainly true in the case of the Black Panthers. The FBI engaged in a deliberate program to disrupt Panther activities that included enhanced surveillance, informants, and infiltration within the group to spread disinformation and cause internal discord. Their methods and the actions of local law enforcement came into question from defense attorneys and judges who believed some of the charges against Panther members had been falsified.

A man peeks around a door that was shot in a police raid at the Balck Panther building in Chicago, 1969

One particularly controversial incident happened in Chicago on December 4, 1969. Police stormed the local Black Panther headquarters, wounded four people, and killed Panthers Mark Clark and Fred Hampton. Officers claimed that an intense gun battle had taken place, but a subsequent investigation determined that all but one of the approximately ninety shots fired came from police weapons. Furthermore, Hampton had been shot in his bed at close range and had not returned fire, suggesting that he had been executed. In 1982, after years of litigation, the survivors were awarded $1.85 million in damages. No charges were ever brought against the police involved in the incident.

The tactics of overzealous law enforcement notwithstanding, many of the difficulties the Panthers found themselves in were of their own making. By the end of the Sixties, the Black Panthers were but a shadow of the political organization that had been founded just three years earlier. Its most prominent leaders were either in jail or on the run from the law. Many chapters gave up their community outreach programs in favor of robbery, drug trafficking, and other illegal activities that they had originally pledged to end in the ghetto. Allen J. Matusow writes, "…many Panthers seemed more interested in crime than in social justice. … Most of the 348 Panther arrests in 1969 stemmed not from politics but from charges of rape, robbery, and burglary."[61]

The Panthers' disintegration into a common street gang alienated all but the radical element of the New Left. The radicals viewed every cop who was killed in a gun battle—and eleven were between 1967 and 1970—as a victory in the war against the Establishment. They romanticized the Black Panthers as revolutionaries, and they wanted to emulate the violent path the Panthers had taken.

SDS Falls Apart

Students for a Democratic Society was having problems of its own in 1969. The organization's original charter rejected a central governing body, and now it was paying the price for that choice. Political factions developed in various SDS chapters, each more radical and leftist than the one before it. Moderate students initially attracted to the organization for its social activism were turned off by the revolutionary rhetoric. Membership dropped off. "So the no-longer-new Left trapped itself in a seamless loop," writes Todd Gitlin, "growing militancy, growing isolation, growing commitment to the Revolution … [and] growing hatred among the competing factions with their competing imaginations."[62]

Another problem was that SDS had focused its energies on universities because of the educational role and social influence they had on American youth. But SDS's founders did not recognize in 1962 that it was impossible to build a sustained movement with university students because they existed in a transitory state. Young people grow older, and their outlook on the world ultimately changes as they are exposed to new experiences. University students eventually graduate and move on with their lives.

These inherent handicaps played a role in the downfall of SDS and its fragmentation into a number of smaller radical groups. At the SDS national convention of June 18–23, 1969, these groups were on full display. Among them was the Progressive Labor party, which consisted of Marxists dedicated to a workers revolution to overthrow the capitalist system in the United States. Labor members were conventional in

Stonewall: Making a Stand for Gay Rights

The Stonewall Inn was a bar in Greenwich Village in New York City that catered to gays and lesbians. In America prior to the modern era, few, if any, public establishments existed where homosexuals could socialize without fear of arrest. Cultural attitudes in America resolutely rejected homosexuality as a disease that was against nature. Anyone who was gay or lesbian generally kept his or her sexuality secret to achieve acceptance in society and sometimes to protect their physical safety.

The police regularly raided the Stonewall, like they did other gay bars, arrested a few people for lewd conduct, and went on their way. A raid on June 28, 1969, turned out different than either law enforcement or patrons could have imagined. A collective feeling of persecution among the patrons expressed itself in a broad resistance to the arrests. Author David Carter describes what happened next: "The first hostile act outside the club occurred when a police officer shoved one of the transvestites, who turned and smacked the officer over the head with her purse. The cop clubbed her, and a wave of anger passed through the crowd." The crowd became increasingly hostile and started throwing pocket change at the police, who then barricaded themselves inside the bar.

"A general assault now began on the Stonewall Inn using anything and everything the crowd outside could get its hands on: garbage, garbage cans, pieces of glass, fire, bricks, cobblestones, and an improvised battering ram were all used to attack the police holed up inside …" The riot gained citywide media attention and afterward homosexuals began organizing in groups to fight for their civil rights. The homosexual lifestyle is much more accepted today than in 1969, but debates still continue over whether gays should be allowed to marry or adopt children.

David Carter, *Stonewall: The Riots that Sparked the Gay Revolution.* New York: St. Martin's, 2004, pps. 148, 160.

style and dress, and they rejected many of the elements of the counterculture. They had infiltrated SDS to seek recruits, and they wanted to use the organization's framework as a base for their own movement.

A faction known as the Revolutionary Youth Movement (RYM) developed in opposition to Progressive Labor, and they subscribed to a broader view of the revolution that encompassed not only workers but also ethnic groups such as the Black Panthers, who were RYM allies. The RYM leadership, which included Mark Rudd, Bill Ayers, and Bernadine Dohrn, wrote a position paper that they circulated at the convention called, "You Don't Need A Weatherman To Know Which Way The Wind Blows," which explained their views. The statement, whose title was drawn from a lyric in a Bob Dylan song, outlined RYM's political ideology and their disagreements with Progressive Labor.

Progressive Labor seized control of the debate at the convention, and RYM walked out and set up its own SDS organization. RYM itself later split into two groups after arguments within its leadership developed over tactics to achieve its goals. RYM II subscribed to the overall revolutionary ideal but not the violent manner in which it would be carried out. The Weathermen, with Ayers, Rudd, and Dohrn, were dedicated to fulfilling the goals of the original RYM document through armed revolution.

This marked the end of SDS as a viable force in the youth movement and the New Left with it. The movement dedicated to participatory democracy and ethnic equality had degenerated into a small group of violent radicals who wanted to tear down the structure of government and society in America.

The Weathermen

The Weathermen, also known as the Weather Underground, wasted no time in starting its revolution. Their numbers were small, so they dispersed to several cities in groups of five to twenty-five members each to recruit people to their cause. They held marathon sessions, during which they preached to new members about the revolutionary struggle. They trained in martial arts to prepare themselves for combat. Total loyalty to the cause was demanded of everyone, and members were encouraged to renounce their possessions, bank accounts, and privacy for the good of the movement. The Weathermen split up couples, because they believed that monogamy was a tool of the Establishment. Everyone was encouraged to have a rotating schedule of different partners regardless of gender or sexual orientation.

The Weathermen were eager to prove their revolutionary zeal, and they often provoked confrontations with local youth in various cities to establish their street credit. They lost many of those fights, but they still claimed victory, because they believed each beating made them stronger. They stormed into high schools to spread their message among students, and they actively encouraged kids to drop out and join them.

During the Days of Rage, the Weathermen spread chaos through Chicago. The public rejected the Weathermen because of their contradictory calls for peace in Vietnam while creating war in American streets.

On October 8, 1969, the Weathermen gathered in Chicago for what they called the Days of Rage. Rudd, Ayers, and Dohrn wanted to bring the war home, and their plan was to spread chaos throughout the city. They called upon and expected thousands to show up, but only three hundred actually came. Undeterred, the Weathermen ran through the streets, smashing windows and vandalizing automobiles. They were intercepted by more than one thousand police officers who waded into the Weathermen and arrested sixty-eight. Two days later the Weathermen charged through the

city's business district and smashed more windows. They were again met by the police. William O'Neill writes, "Hardly a Weatherman was left unbooked."[63]

The actions of the Weathermen did not impress anyone. The students who had formerly belonged to SDS, the Black Panthers, and the public at large all rejected the Weathermen because of their contradictory calls for peace in Vietnam and war in the streets of America. The general criticism was that they were engaging in vandalism, not revolution. Their violent rhetoric was not having any positive effect on the movement.

Easy Rider Defines a Generation

Motion pictures in the late 1960s became more daring and inventive in an attempt to capture younger audiences. Producers turned to young writers and directors for ideas that spoke to their generation. In 1968 two such filmmakers, Dennis Hopper and Peter Fonda, were given a $500,000 budget to make a road movie about a pair of young men who ride their motorcycles from California to New Orleans to celebrate Mardi Gras. As writer Jeff Stafford explains:

> ... [T]he film is much more than that and shows a diverse cross section of American culture that encompasses lifestyle experimentation (the hippie commune), intolerance (the hostile locals at a backwater Louisiana diner), and wanderlust (the motorcycle becomes a symbol for freedom). It is the ultimate "road trip" movie and even though it ends in tragedy, the movie celebrates the natural beauty of rural America in a startlingly fresh way, juxtaposing the two cyclists against stunning landscapes and ever-changing vistas on their journey.
>
> Most importantly, *Easy Rider* represented a crossroads in the film industry, one where the old Hollywood system had become stagnant while young filmmakers were revitalizing the medium with fresh, creative ideas that were having a real impact on the culture and their generation.
>
> *Easy Rider* was released in 1969 to critical praise and box office success. It received two Academy Award nominations and launched the careers of Hopper, Fonda, and co-star Jack Nicholson. It is widely considered to be one of the best American films ever made.

Jeff Stafford, "American Film Revolution of the '60s and '70s," Turner Classic Movies. http://www.tcm.com/thismonth/article/?cid=188869.

Ayers and Dohrn and several cohorts were undeterred and expanded their campaign of disruption to include random acts of arson, property destruction, and bombings that lasted well into the 1970s. They targeted banks in several cities, U.S. post offices, military offices, and even the U.S. Capitol building in Washington, D.C.

On March 6, 1970, three Weathermen were killed in a Greenwich Village home when a bomb they were preparing accidentally exploded. After this the Weathermen went underground and remained in hiding for several years. Ayers and Dohrn turned themselves in to authorities in 1980. They became professors with respected reputations in Chicago despite never having renounced their actions as leaders of the Weather Underground. In 2001 Ayers commented, "I don't regret setting bombs ... I feel we didn't do enough."[64]

Woodstock: Hope Emerges

Amidst the turmoil stirred up by the Weathermen and the Black Panthers, the youth of the counterculture continued to embrace the free attitudes they had espoused throughout the decade. Hippies still wandered the country, and the style of dress and music of the counterculture had become popular among a broad cross section of the nation's youth. On August 15, 1969, between 300,000 and 400,000 of them congregated in Bethel, New York, to attend the Woodstock Music and Arts Fair.

The three-day event was planned by a small group of promoters and investors who were interested in hosting a concert to coincide with the opening of a recording studio in nearby Woodstock, New York. The promoters secured 600 acres from farmer Max Yasgur for the festival site, and they signed up thirty-two performing acts, including Joan Baez, Richie Havens, Arlo Guthrie, the Grateful Dead, Janis Joplin, the Who, Jimi Hendrix, and others. Attendance was expected to reach about 150,000. By Thursday, August 14, 30,000 people had already arrived.

It became apparent early into the concert that the crowd would exceed the promoters' wildest expectations. They initially charged $18 (approximately $75 adjusted for inflation), but as the crowd swelled to more than 300,000, people tore down the fences and made their way in past a security team that was overwhelmed by the crowds.

Food and water ran out, toilets backed up, sanitation was poor, and the medical facilities were woefully inadequate. The New York State Thruway was backed up for hours, and people abandoned their cars and proceeded to the concert on foot. Musicians and supplies had to be flown in by helicopter. Then it started raining, turning the fields into seas of mud. An announcer addressed the crowd on the first night, "We're going to need each other to help each other work this out, because we're taxing the systems that we've set up. ... The one major thing that you have to remember tonight is that the man next to you is your brother."[65]

Bethel residents helped out by providing food and showers for concert attendees. Police and emergency services personnel did their best to keep the situation from deteriorating into chaos. New York Governor Nelson Rockefeller was persuaded against sending in the National Guard, because the promoters feared it would upset the attendees. The festival went off remarkably well considering the circumstances. *Life* magazine noted, "For three days nearly half a million people lived elbow to elbow in the most exposed, crowded, rain-drenched, uncomfortable kind of community and there wasn't so much as a fist-fight."[66]

It's hard to say how long this camaraderie would have lasted if the attendees

The Woodstock Music and Arts fair in Bethel, New York attracted nearly a half-million people. Despite overcrowding, poor sanitation, and backed up toilets, it was a peaceful event.

The Counterculture Loses Its Way ■ 79

had to endure more than two or three days of such adverse conditions. The event was considered a success just the same, and it became a seminal moment both in the world of music and in the history of the counterculture. The best qualities of the young generation were on display—community, peace, and brotherhood—and many believed that if the mindset of Woodstock could be duplicated, the world would be a better place.

Altamont: Hope Fades

The Rolling Stones were impressed by what took place at Woodstock, and they planned their own music festival in

Hell's Angels

A group of motorcycle enthusiasts who preferred to live outside society started the Hell's Angels Motorcycle Club in California in the late 1940s. The group maintained a strict code of secrecy, so little information was known about their background and the extent of their membership. They gained an unsavory reputation for their unkempt appearance, their uninhibited partying lifestyle, and their criminal activities. They boasted numerous chapters across the country and overseas, but in the Sixties the Oakland chapter led by Ralph "Sonny" Barger was the most well known. Historian William L. O'Neill explains:

> The publicity given this small band of hoodlums had strange consequences. Although the Oakland Angels had no more than eighty-five members, they were certified as a Grade A national menace by the press. ... And for a time they won the favor of the New Left intellectuals and thrill-seekers—partly, no doubt, because their violent lives appealed to the growing strain of revolutionary machismo. ...

> This was a mistake. Though rebellious, the motorcycle outlaws had more in common with the radical right than the radical left. They were all instinctive fascists, insanely patriotic, and anti-communist to the bone.

> Federal and state law enforcement agencies battled with the Angels on and off for years, but the organization still exists, with more than one hundred chapters in twenty-nine countries.

William L. O'Neill, *Coming Apart: An Informal History of America in the 1960s*. New York: Times Books, 1971, pps. 273–274.

California to close their American tour. The Altamont Speedway Free Festival, scheduled for December 6, 1969, included musical groups Santana, Jefferson Airplane, Crosby, Stills & Nash, and the Rolling Stones as the final act.

The event, which promoters imagined as a Woodstock West, was poorly planned, and the 300,000 attendees endured an inadequate number of portable toilets, a shortage of medical services, and, for the hippies, bad acid. Additionally, the Hells Angels motorcycle gang, who had been hired to keep people off the stage for the price of $500 worth of beer, got into numerous altercations with the crowd and some of the bands. They were armed with sawed-off pool cues and they used them liberally on a number of people who either got too close to the stage or too close to their bikes.

Grace Slick of the Jefferson Airplane called for everyone, including the Angels, to act more civilized after witnessing one such beating during the band's set. Guitarist Marty Balin was knocked unconscious by one of the Angels when he tried to intercede.

By the time the Rolling Stones took the stage that evening, the crowd had grown increasingly intoxicated, restless, and irritated. A number of fights broke out among attendees and between attendees and Angels. Rolling Stones lead singer Mick Jagger watched fights break out in the crowd in front of the stage, and he interrupted his performance a number of times asking people to calm down. While the band performed their recent hit, "Sympathy for the Devil," Meredith Hunter, a young black man in the crowd, pulled a gun after being punched in the face by one of the Angels. A group of Hells Angels ganged up on him, and he was stabbed and beaten to death in full view of the band and many onlookers. An autopsy revealed that Hunter had methamphetamine in his system. Biker Alan Passaro was charged with Hunter's murder, but he was later acquitted on grounds of self-defense.

The incident was caught on film for a documentary the Rolling Stones were making of their American tour called "Gimme Shelter." The Hells Angels accused the Stones of poor planning and of blaming them for the violence that took place at Altamont. Many viewed the entire event as a tragic affair. Terry Anderson writes, "A cultural activist wrote that the concert 'exploded the myth of innocent,' and many other underground writers felt that Altamont signaled 'The Failure of the Counterculture.' ... it was the 'last gasp from a dying decade.'"[67]

Legacy of the Counterculture

The rise and fall of the counterculture of the Sixties left a mixed legacy for the decade. This was due in large part to the various elements that made up the counterculture and the diverse agendas of university students, blacks, women, hippies, and radicals. Their goals sometimes overlapped, particularly with regard to their desire to end the Vietnam War and make lasting changes that would end what they perceived to be the Establishment's stranglehold on the country. Even

The estimated 10 million people that took part in thousands of antiwar demonstrations contributed to the most extensive social activism in American history.

then, however, they differed on what tactics to employ to achieve those goals.

Political commentators Lynn Scarlett and Michael Barone point out that the politics embraced by the youth of the '60s was "a collection of paradoxes: denouncing authority but obsessed with power; speaking of the dignity of individuals but preoccupied with group rights; proclaiming the virtues of personal empowerment but finding victims everywhere; at once decentralizing and centralizing; trusting in the rational plan but eschewing formal organizations."[68] These contradictions contributed to the confusion that ultimately toppled SDS and, by decade's end, alienated a number of dedicated young men and women involved in the student movement.

On a more positive note, the Sixties witnessed the most widespread and sustained social activism in American history. An estimated 10 million people took part in thousands of antiwar demonstrations, although their effect on America's involvement in the Vietnam War is debatable. The war continued until 1973 regardless of the continued protests, but American politicians carefully weighed the costs and benefits of future military engagements, wary of repeating the mistakes that drew millions of protesters into the streets during the Sixties.

The civil rights movement had a more tangible record of success, inspiring new laws that brought an end to institutionalized racism and segregation. Through the rest of the twentieth century, blacks in America made continuous economic gains, and they also experienced a wider array of educational and career opportunities. In 2008 the United States elected its first black president, an event considered an improbability forty years prior.

The social activism practiced by the baby boomers in the Sixties continued in subsequent decades in the shape of crusades to clean up the environment, achieve gender equality, and reduce violent crime. Politicians and judges became more sensitive to the rights of minorities and ethnic groups to ensure that all people would have equal access to better jobs and living standards. Government programs, such as affirmative action and the redrawing of congressional districts to increase minority-voting blocs that would elect minority representatives, drew controversy that continues to this day. Supporters of these efforts claim that they are necessary to correct the decades of racism that stifled opportunities among minority groups. Detractors maintain that these programs do not offer equal opportunity but instead rely on preferential treatment that keeps minorities reliant on government resources and perpetuates reverse discrimination.

The counterculture of the Sixties left an indelible impression on music and the arts in America, inspiring future generations of musicians, writers, and filmmakers. Conservative boundaries were forever broken, and, whereas some artists exploited that fact merely for shock value, others took the opportunity to tackle meaningful and controversial subjects that evoked debate and serious thought about social issues. The fashions of the time also still resonate as each subsequent generation that has followed the baby boomers adapts some element of dress, hairstyle, or terminology that keep the spirit of the decade alive.

The Sixties meant many things to many people, and continued fascination with the time results in constantly evolving definitions and analyses. Those who lived through that decade cannot always agree on whether it was a decade of progress or devastation, high hopes or shattered dreams, a break from a conformist past or a leap into an uncertain future. In reality, the Sixties and the counterculture that shaped it is a mix of all these things. Americans were at their best, and they were at their worst. Bob Dylan, whose words so effectively captured the feelings of the decade, may have said it best: "It was like a flying saucer landed. That's what the Sixties were like. Everybody heard about it, but only a few really saw it."[69]

Notes

Introduction: Marching to a Different Beat

1. Joyce Johnson, "Remembering Jack Kerouac," *Smithsonian* Magazine, September 2007, http://www.smithsonianmag.com/arts-culture/music-literature/tribute_kerouac.html.
2. Quoted in Christopher Gair, *The American Counterculture*. Edinburgh: Edinburgh University Press, 2007, p. 40.

Chapter One: Exploring a New Frontier

3. Quoted in William Safire, *Lend Me Your Ears: Great Speeches in History*. New York: W.W. Norton, 2004, p. 970.
4. Quoted in Terry H. Anderson, *The Movement and the Sixties: Protest in American from Greensboro to Wounded Knee*. New York: Oxford University Press, 1995, p. 59.
5. Quoted in James Miller, *Democracy Is in the Streets: From Port Huron to the Siege of Chicago*. Cambridge: Harvard University Press, 1987, p. 47.
6. Allen J. Matusow, *The Unraveling of America: A History of Liberalism in the 1960s*. New York: Harper & Row, 1984, p. 295.
7. Joseph Heller, *Catch-22*. New York: Simon & Schuster, 1961, p. 46.
8. William H. Whyte, *The Organization Man*. Philadelphia: University of Pennsylvania Press, 1956, p. 68.
9. Rachel Carson, *Silent Spring*. New York: Houghton Mifflin, 1962, p. 7.
10. C. Wright Mills, *The Power Elite*. New York: Oxford University Press, 1956, p. 294.
11. Anderson, *The Movement and the Sixties*, p. 62.
12. Quoted in Miller, *Democracy Is in the Streets*, p. 373.
13. Todd Gitlin, *The Sixties: Years of Hope, Days of Rage*. New York: Bantam, 1987, p. 85.
14. James Farmer, *Lay Bare the Heart: An Autobiography of the Civil Rights Movement*. New York: Penguin, 1985, p. 206.
15. JFK in History: Civil Rights Context in the Early 1960s, "Radio and Television Report to the American People on Civil Rights, June 11, 1963," John Kennedy speech, the White House, John F. Kennedy Presidential Library & Museum, June 11, 1963. http://www.jfklibrary.org/Historical+Resources/JFK+in+History/Civil+Rights+Context+in+the+Early+1960s+Page+4.htm.
16. Quoted in Safire, *Lend Me Your Ears*, p. 564.
17. Matusow, *The Unraveling of America*, p. 14.

Chapter Two: Raising the Stakes

18. Lyndon Baines Johnson, *The Vantage Point: Perspectives of the Presidency, 1963–1969*. New York: Holt, Rinehart and Winston, 1971, p. 104.
19. John Coplans, "Early Warhol: The Systematic Evolution of the Impersonal Style." *Artforum*, March 1970, p. 59.
20. William L. O'Neill, *Coming Apart: An Informal History of America in the 1960s*. New York: Times Books, 1971, p. 204.
21. Gitlin, *The Sixties*, p. 207.
22. O'Neill, *Coming Apart*, p. 205.
23. Lenny Bruce, "Famous Quotes," The Official Lenny Bruce Web site. http://www.lennybruceofficial.com/famous-quotes.
24. Quoted in Matusow, *The Unraveling of America*, p. 317.
25. Quoted in Anderson, *The Movement and the Sixties*, p. 87.
26. Quoted in David Lance Goines, *The Free Speech Movement: Coming of Age in the 1960s*. Berkeley: Ten Speed, 1993, p. 361.
27. Quoted in Goines, *The Free Speech Movement*, p. 466.
28. Betty Friedan, *The Feminine Mystique*. New York: W.W. Norton, 1963, p. 79.
29. Quoted in James T. Patterson, *Grand Expectations: The United States, 1945–1974*. New York: Oxford University Press, p. 645.
30. Casey Hayden and Mary King, "Sex and Caste: A Kind of Memo," Mary E. King Web site, http://www.maryking.info/Mary-King-Sex-and-Caste-Memo.html.
31. Johnson, *The Vantage Point*, p. 160.
32. Quoted in American Experience, "Malcolm X: Making It Plain," PBS, May 19, 2005. http://www.pbs.org/wgbh/amex/malcolmx/timeline/timeline2.html.
33. Malcolm X, *The Autobiography of Malcolm X: as Told to Alex Haley*. New York: Ballantine, 1999, p. 307.
34. Quoted in Patterson, *Grand Expectations*, p. 581.
35. Quoted in Patterson, *Grand Expectations*, p. 480.

Chapter Three: Turning On, Tuning In, Dropping Out

36. Gitlin, *The Sixties*, p. 19.
37. Quoted in Anderson, *The Movement and the Sixties*, p. 244.
38. "Overview: Who Were (Are) the Diggers?" The Digger Archives, July 17, 2009. http://www.diggers.org/overview.htm.
39. Quoted in Burton H. Wolfe, *The Hippies*. New York: New American Library, 1968, p. 13.
40. Matusow, *The Unraveling of America*, p. 302.
41. Stewart Brand, "The Purpose of the Whole Earth Catalog," *The Whole Earth Catalog*, Fall 1968.
42. Quoted in Anderson, *The Movement and the Sixties*, p. 148.
43. Quoted in David M. Barrett, *Uncertain Warriors: Lyndon Johnson and His Vietnam Advisers*. Lawrence: University Press of Kansas, 1993, p. 81.
44. Paul Lyons, "Another Sixties: The New Right," The Sixties Project, March 1993. http://www2.iath.virginia.edu/sixties/HTML_docs/Texts/Scholarly/Lyons_Another_60s_01.html.

45. Marc Jason Gilbert, ed. *The Vietnam War on Campus: Other Voices, More Distant Drums*. Westport: Praeger, 2001, p. 2.

46. Quoted in Anderson, *The Movement and the Sixties*, p. 255.

Chapter Four: From Protest to Resistance

47. Gitlin, *The Sixties*, p. 256.

48. Quoted in Matusow, *The Unraveling of America*, p. 330.

49. Quoted in W. J. Rorabaugh, *Berkeley at War: The 1960s*. New York: Oxford University Press, 1989, p. 105.

50. Stewart Burns, *Social Movements of the 1960s: Searching for Democracy*. New York: Twayne, 1990, p. 86.

51. Quoted in Miller, *Democracy Is in the Streets*, p. 293.

52. Maurice Briton, "Paris: May 1968—Maurice Brinton's diary," Libcom. org, July 22, 2005. http://libcom. org/library/May-68-Solidarity.

53. Quoted in Jan Puhl, "The Tragic Failure of the Prague Spring," *Spiegel International*, April 7, 2008. http://www.spiegel.de/international/europe/0,1518,563951,00. html

54. Quoted in Burns, *Social Movements of the 1960s*, p. 42.

55. Quoted in Matusow, *The Unraveling of America*, p. 355.

56. Patterson, *Grand Expectations*, p. 662.

57. Quoted in *Speeches That Changed the World: The Stories and Transcripts of the Moments That Made History*. London: Smith Davies, 2006, p 155.

58. Quoted in Gilbert, *The Vietnam War on Campus*, p. 58.

59. Judith Clavir Albert and Stewart Edward Albert, *The Sixties Papers: Documents of a Rebellious Decade*. Westport, Praeger, 1984, p. 34.

Chapter Five: The Counterculture Loses Its Way

60. Quoted in Gitlin, *The Sixties*, p. 314.

61. Matusow, *The Unraveling of America*, p. 373.

62. Gitlin, *The Sixties*, p. 381.

63. O'Neill, *Coming Apart*, p. 297.

64. Quoted in Harvey Klehr, "Fugitive Days by Bill Ayers," Commentary, December 2001, http://www.commentarymagazine.com/viewarticle.cfm/fugitive-days-by-bill-ayers-9400.

65. Quoted in Anderson, *The Movement and the Sixties*, p. 278.

66. "The Woodstock Rock Trip," *Life*, August 29, 1969, p. 14.

67. Quoted in Anderson, *The Movement and the Sixties*, p. 282.

68. Lynn Scarlett and Michael Barone, "Missing the Boat? Was the '60s Disdain for Bigness, Centralization, & Conformity Healthy Until It Went Awry?" *The American Enterprise*, May-June 1997.

69. Quoted in James Miller, *Almost Grown: The Rise of Rock and Roll*. London: Arrow, 2000, p. 312.

For Further Reading

Books

American Heritage Illustrated History of the United States, Volume 17: The Vietnam Era. New York: Choice, 1988. An illustrated history of the Vietnam War and the anti-war movement in the United States.

Rachel Carson, *Silent Spring*. New York: Houghton Mifflin, 1962. Details the harm that pollution and synthetic chemicals cause to the environment; considered the cornerstone of the modern environmental movement.

David Farber and Beth Bailey, *The Columbia Guide to America in the 1960s*. New York: Columbia University Press, 2001. Historical accounts, charts, statistics, chronologies, and essays of the Sixties.

James Farmer, *Lay Bare the Heart: An Autobiography of the Civil Rights Movement*. New York: Penguin, 1985. A history of the civil rights movement by one of its most prominent activists.

Betty Friedan, *The Feminine Mystique*. New York: W.W. Norton, 1963. Freidan's book explored the status of women in post–World War II society and became required reading for the feminist movement.

Sandra Gurvis, *Where Have All the Flower Children Gone?* Jackson: University Press of Mississippi, 2006. A series of interviews with several people who came of age during the Sixties, exploring their roles at the time and their views today.

Neil A. Hamilton, *The ABC-CLIO Companion to the 1960s Counterculture in America*. Santa Barbara, CA: ABC-CLIO, 1997. An encyclopedia of the events, people, and movements of the 1960s counterculture.

Micah L. Issitt, *Hippies: A Guide to an American Subculture*. Santa Barbara, CA: ABC-CLIO, 2009. A comprehensive introduction to hippie culture including a chronology and biographies.

Brian Ward, ed., *The 1960s: A Documentary Reader*. West Sussex, United Kingdom: John Wiley & Sons, 2009. A collection of primary documents from the decade, including speeches, photographs, song lyrics, court decisions, and other materials.

Web Sites

The Digger Archives (http://www.diggers.org). A history of the San Francisco Diggers, including a chronology of important events of the Sixties, essays, photographs, and more.

Multimedia Sixties (http://www.sixties60s.com/). A year-by-year chronology of the Sixties that explores social, culture, political, and entertainment events of the decade.

The Sixties: The Years That Shaped a Generation (http://www.pbs.org/opb/thesixties/index.html). Resource site that is a companion to the PBS documentary series, including interviews, biographical sketches of newsmakers, and a resource library.

The Sixties Project (http://www2.iath.virginia.edu/sixties/HTML_docs/Sixties.html). A scholarly collection of essays, interviews, and personal histories from the time period.

The Summer of Love: The American Experience (http://www.pbs.org/wgbh/amex/love/index.html). An information source of the PBS documentary, including chronologies, interviews, and video clips from the documentary.

The Whole World Was Watching: An Oral History of 1968 (http://www.stg.brown.edu/projects/1968/). The Scholarly Technology Group at Brown University assembled this collection of interviews and reference materials from 1968, the most turbulent year of the decade.

Woodstock Story (http://www.woodstockstory.com/). A collection of photographs, stories, artwork, and other items from the 1969 Woodstock Music and Arts Festival.

Index

Democratic National Convention (1968), 69
Selma to Montgomery March, 40
Stonewall riot, 74
University of California, Berkeley demonstration, 19
Politics, 82
Pop art, 28, *29*, 30
The Port Huron Statement (Students for a Democratic Society), 18–19, 26
Post World War II era, 14
The Power Elite (Wright), 16–17
Prague Spring, 63
Pranksters, 30, *31*
Presidential primary (1968), 56–57
Progressive Labor Party, 74–75
Psychology, 35

R
Race riots, *40*, 41
Racial discrimination, 20–24, 38–40
Radicalism
    Students for a Democratic Society (SDS), 56
    Weathermen, 75–78
    Yippies, 68–69
    See also Militancy
Radicals, 57–61, 73
Randolph, A. Philip, 23
Ray, James Earl, 67
Revolutionary ideals, 57–59, 75–78
Revolutionary Youth Movement (RYM), 75
Riots
    King assassination, reaction to the, 67
    1967, 56
    Stonewall riots, 74
    University of Mississippi integration, 22–23
    Watts neighborhood, *40*, 41
Rock music. *See* Music
Rolling Stones, 80–81
Rubin, Jerry, *68*, 68–69
Rudd, Mark, 60, 75, 76

S
San Francisco, California, 30, 44–48, 52
San Francisco Mime Troupe, *52*
Savio, Mario, 33–35
SDS. *See* Students for a Democratic Society (SDS)
Seale, Bobby, 65
Segregation, 20, 22, 38, 60
Selma to Montgomery march, 39–40
Sexism, 36–37
Sharon Statement, 53
Silent Spring (Carson), 16
Sirhan, Sirhan, 67
Sit-ins, 20, *21*
Slick, Grace, 81
Smith, Tommie, 66, *66*
Social issues, 82–83
Sociology, 16–17
Southern States, 38
Soviet Union, 63
Spock, Benjamin, 35
Sproul Hall, 34
Stender, Marvin, 52
Stonewall riots, 74
Stop the Draft Week, 51, 53
Street theater, 45
Strikes, labor, 43
Student Afro Society (SAS), 60
Student Nonviolent Coordinating Committee (SNCC), 63–64
Students. *See* College students
Students for a Democratic Society (SDS)
    antiwar movement, 51
    Columbia University protest, 60–61
    conflict within, 70, 72
    downfall of, 73–75
    formation, 18–20
    Oakland Army Terminal demonstration, 35
    radicalism and violence, 56
    sexism, 37
Summer of Love, *44*, 47–48

Picture Credits

About the Author

This is Richard Brownell's sixth title for Lucent Books. His other books include *The Fall of the Confederacy and the End of Slavery* and *America's Failure in Vietnam*, which are part of Lucent's History's Great Defeats series; *The Oklahoma City Bombing*, which is part of Lucent's Crime Scene Investigation Series; *Immigration*, part of the Hot Topics series; and The Cold War, part of the American History series. He is a published playwright with several stage productions to his credit. He also writes political commentary for various periodicals and Internet sites. He holds a Bachelor of Fine Arts degree from New York University. Richard lives in New York City.